MW01104956

GENOCIDE & PERSECUTION

Liberia

Titles in the Genocide and Persecution Series

Afghanistan
Argentina
Armenia
Bosnia
Burma
Cambodia
Chile
Darfur
East Pakistan
El Salvador and Guatemala
The Holocaust
Indonesia
Kosovo
The Kurds
Liberia
Namibia
The People's Republic of China
The Romani
Russia
Rwanda
South Africa
Sri Lanka
Tibet
Uganda

GENOCIDE & PERSECUTION

Liberia

Noah Berlatsky
Book Editor

Frank Chalk
Consulting Editor

GREENHAVEN PRESS
A part of Gale, Cengage Learning

GALE
CENGAGE Learning·

Farmington Hills, Mich • San Francisco • New York • Waterville, Maine
Meriden, Conn • Mason, Ohio • Chicago

Elizabeth Des Chenes, *Director, Content Strategy*
Cynthia Sanner, *Publisher*
Douglas Dentino, *Manager, New Product*

© 2014 Greenhaven Press, a part of Gale, Cengage Learning

WCN: 01-100-101

Gale and Greenhaven Press are registered trademarks used herein under license.

For more information, contact:
Greenhaven Press
27500 Drake Rd.
Farmington Hills, MI 48331-3535
Or you can visit our Internet site at gale.cengage.com.

ALL RIGHTS RESERVED
No part of this work covered by the copyright herein may be reproduced, transmitted, stored, or used in any form or by any means graphic, electronic, or mechanical, including but not limited to photocopying, recording, scanning, digitizing, taping, Web distribution, information networks, or information storage and retrieval systems, except as permitted under Section 107 or 108 of the 1976 United States Copyright Act, without the prior written permission of the publisher.

For product information and technology assistance, contact us at:

Gale Customer Support, 1-800-877-4253
For permission to use material from this text or product, submit all requests online at www.cengage.com/permissions.

Further permissions questions can be emailed to permissionrequest@cengage.com.

Every effort is made to ensure that Greenhaven Press accurately reflects the original intent of the authors. Every effort has been made to trace the owners of copyrighted material.

Cover Image Credit: © Patrick Robert/Sygma/Corbis.
Interior barbed wire artwork © f9photos, used under license from Shutterstock.com.

LIBRARY OF CONGRESS CATALOGING-IN-PUBLICATION DATA

Liberia / Noah Berlatsky, book editor.
     pages cm. -- (Genocide and persecution)
     Includes bibliographical references and index.
     ISBN 978-0-7377-6899-2 (hardcover)
1. Liberia--History--1980- 2. Liberia--Politics and government--1980- 3. Political violence--Liberia. 4. Crimes against humanity--Liberia. 5. Child soldiers--Liberia. 6. Human rights--Liberia. I. Berlatsky, Noah, editor of compilation. II. Series: Genocide and persecution.
     DT636.5.L498 2014
     966.6203--dc23   2014000754

Printed in the United States of America
1 2 3 4 5 6 7 18 17 16 15 14

Contents

A journalist argues that the Truth and Reconciliation Report will open old wounds and exacerbate antagonisms and divisions in the country.

Chapter 3: Personal Narratives

Preface

*"For the dead and the living, we must
  bear witness."*

> Elie Wiesel, Nobel laureate and
> Holocaust survivor

The histories of many nations are shaped by horrific events involving torture, violent repression, and systematic mass killings. The inhumanity of such events is difficult to comprehend, yet understanding why such events take place, what impact they have on society, and how they may be prevented in the future is vitally important. The Genocide and Persecution series provides readers with anthologies of previously published materials on acts of genocide, crimes against humanity, and other instances of extreme persecution, with an emphasis on events taking place in the twentieth and twenty-first centuries. The series offers essential historical background on these significant events in modern world history, presents the issues and controversies surrounding the events, and provides first-person narratives from people whose lives were altered by the events. By providing primary sources, as well as analysis of crucial issues, these volumes help develop critical-thinking skills and support global connections. In addition, the series directly addresses curriculum standards focused on informational text and literary nonfiction and explicitly promotes literacy in history and social studies.

Each Genocide and Persecution volume focuses on genocide, crimes against humanity, or severe persecution. Material from a variety of primary and secondary sources presents a multinational perspective on the event. Articles are carefully edited and introduced to provide context for readers. The series includes volumes on significant and widely studied events like the Holocaust, as well as events that are less often studied, such as the East Pakistan genocide in what is now Bangladesh. Some volumes focus on multiple events endured by a specific people, such as the Kurds, or multiple events enacted over time by a particular oppressor or in a particular location, such as the People's Republic of China.

Each volume is organized into three chapters. The first chapter provides readers with general background information and uses primary sources such as testimony from tribunals or international courts, documents or speeches from world leaders, and legislative text. The second chapter presents multinational perspectives on issues and controversies and addresses current implications or long-lasting effects of the event. Viewpoints explore such topics as root causes; outside interventions, if any; the impact on the targeted group and the region; and the contentious issues that arose in the aftermath. The third chapter presents first-person narratives from affected people, including survivors, family members of victims, perpetrators, officials, aid workers, and other witnesses.

In addition, numerous features are included in each volume of Genocide and Persecution:

- An annotated **table of contents** provides a brief summary of each essay in the volume.
- A **foreword** gives important background information on the recognition, definition, and study of genocide in recent history and examines current efforts focused on the prevention of future atrocities.
- A **chronology** offers important dates leading up to, during, and following the event.
- **Primary sources**—including historical newspaper accounts, testimony, and personal narratives—are among the varied selections in the anthology.
- **Illustrations**—including a world map, photographs, charts, graphs, statistics, and tables—are closely tied

to the text and chosen to help readers understand key points or concepts.

- **Sidebars**—including biographies of key figures and overviews of earlier or related historical events—offer additional content.
- **Pedagogical features**—including analytical exercises, writing prompts, and group activities—introduce each chapter and help reinforce the material. These features promote proficiency in writing, speaking, and listening skills and literacy in history and social studies.
- A **glossary** defines key terms, as needed.
- An annotated list of international **organizations to contact** presents sources of additional information on the volume topic.
- A **list of primary source documents** provides an annotated list of reports, treaties, resolutions, and judicial decisions related to the volume topic.
- A **for further research** section offers a bibliography of books, periodical articles, and Internet sources and an annotated section of other items such as films and websites.
- A comprehensive subject **index** provides access to key people, places, events, and subjects cited in the text.

The Genocide and Persecution series illuminates atrocities that cannot and should not be forgotten. By delving deeply into these events from a variety of perspectives, students and other readers are provided with the information they need to think critically about the past and its implications for the future.

Foreword

The term *genocide* often appears in news stories and other literature. It is not widely known, however, that the core meaning of the term comes from a legal definition, and the concept became part of international criminal law only in 1951 when the United Nations Convention on the Prevention and Punishment of the Crime of Genocide came into force. The word *genocide* appeared in print for the first time in 1944 when Raphael Lemkin, a Polish Jewish refugee from Adolf Hitler's World War II invasion of Eastern Europe, invented the term and explored its meaning in his pioneering book *Axis Rule in Occupied Europe.*

Humanity's Recognition of Genocide and Persecution

Lemkin understood that throughout the history of the human race there have always been leaders who thought they could solve their problems not only through victory in war, but also by destroying entire national, ethnic, racial, or religious groups. Such annihilations of entire groups, in Lemkin's view, deprive the world of the very cultural diversity and richness in languages, traditions, values, and practices that distinguish the human race from all other life on earth. Genocide is not only unjust, it threatens the very existence and progress of human civilization, in Lemkin's eyes.

Looking to the past, Lemkin understood that the prevailing coarseness and brutality of earlier human societies and the lower value placed on human life obscured the existence of genocide. Sacrifice and exploitation, as well as torture and public execution, had been common at different times in history. Looking toward a more humane future, Lemkin asserted the need to punish— and when possible prevent—a crime for which there had been no name until he invented it.

Legal Definitions of Genocide

On December 9, 1948, the United Nations adopted its Convention on the Prevention and Punishment of the Crime of Genocide (UNGC). Under Article II, genocide

> means any of the following acts committed with intent to destroy, in whole or in part, a national, ethnical, racial or religious group, as such:
>
> (a) Killing members of the group;
>
> (b) Causing serious bodily or mental harm to members of the group;
>
> (c) Deliberately inflicting on the group conditions of life calculated to bring about its physical destruction in whole or in part;
>
> (d) Imposing measures intended to prevent births within the group;
>
> (e) Forcibly transferring children of the group to another group.

Article III of the convention defines the elements of the crime of genocide, making punishable:

> (a) Genocide;
>
> (b) Conspiracy to commit genocide;
>
> (c) Direct and public incitement to commit genocide;
>
> (d) Attempt to commit genocide;
>
> (e) Complicity in genocide.

After intense debate, the architects of the convention excluded acts committed with intent to destroy social, political, and economic groups from the definition of genocide. Thus, attempts to destroy whole social classes—the physically and mentally challenged, and homosexuals, for example—are not acts of genocide under the terms of the UNGC. These groups achieved a belated but very significant measure of protection under international criminal law in the Rome Statute of the International Criminal

Court, adopted at a conference on July 17, 1998, and entered into force on July 1, 2002.

The Rome Statute defined a crime against humanity in the following way:

> any of the following acts when committed as part of a widespread and systematic attack directed against any civilian population:
>
> (a) Murder;
>
> (b) Extermination;
>
> (c) Enslavement;
>
> (d) Deportation or forcible transfer of population;
>
> (e) Imprisonment or other severe deprivation of physical liberty in violation of fundamental rules of international law;
>
> (f) Torture;
>
> (g) Rape, sexual slavery, enforced prostitution, forced pregnancy, enforced sterilization, or any other form of sexual violence of comparable gravity;
>
> (h) Persecution against any identifiable group or collectivity on political, racial, national, ethnic, cultural, religious, gender . . . or other grounds that are universally recognized as impermissible under international law, in connection with any act referred to in this paragraph or any crime within the jurisdiction of this Court;
>
> (i) Enforced disappearance of persons;
>
> (j) The crime of apartheid;
>
> (k) Other inhumane acts of a similar character intentionally causing great suffering, or serious injury to body or to mental or physical health.

Although genocide is often ranked as "the crime of crimes," in practice prosecutors find it much easier to convict perpetrators of crimes against humanity rather than genocide under domestic laws. However, while Article I of the UNGC declares that countries adhering to the UNGC recognize genocide as "a crime under international law which they undertake to prevent and to punish," the Rome Statute provides no comparable international mechanism for the prosecution of crimes against humanity. A treaty would help individual countries and international institutions introduce measures to prevent crimes against humanity, as well as open more avenues to the domestic and international prosecution of war criminals.

The Evolving Laws of Genocide

In the aftermath of the serious crimes committed against civilians in the former Yugoslavia since 1991 and the Rwanda genocide of 1994, the United Nations Security Council created special international courts to bring the alleged perpetrators of these events to justice. While the UNGC stands as the standard definition of genocide in law, the new courts contributed significantly to today's nuanced meaning of genocide, crimes against humanity, ethnic cleansing, and serious war crimes in international criminal law.

Also helping to shape contemporary interpretations of such mass atrocity crimes are the special and mixed courts for Sierra Leone, Cambodia, Lebanon, and Iraq, which may be the last of their type in light of the creation of the International Criminal Court (ICC), with its broad jurisdiction over mass atrocity crimes in all countries that adhere to the Rome Statute of the ICC. The Yugoslavia and Rwanda tribunals have already clarified the law of genocide, ruling that rape can be prosecuted as a weapon in committing genocide, evidence of intent can be absent when convicting low-level perpetrators of genocide, and public incitement to commit genocide is a crime even if genocide does not immediately follow the incitement.

Several current controversies about genocide are worth noting and will require more research in the future:

1. Dictators accused of committing genocide or persecution may hold onto power more tightly for fear of becoming

vulnerable to prosecution after they step down. Therefore, do threats of international indictments of these alleged perpetrators actually delay transfers of power to more representative rulers, thereby causing needless suffering?

2. Would the large sum of money spent for international retributive justice be better spent on projects directly benefiting the survivors of genocide and persecution?

3. Can international courts render justice impartially or do they deliver only "victors' justice," that is the application of one set of rules to judge the vanquished and a different and laxer set of rules to judge the victors?

It is important to recognize that the law of genocide is constantly evolving, and scholars searching for the roots and early warning signs of genocide may prefer to use their own definitions of genocide in their work. While the UNGC stands as the standard definition of genocide in law, the debate over its interpretation and application will never end. The ultimate measure of the value of any definition of genocide is its utility for identifying the roots of genocide and preventing future genocides.

Motives for Genocide and Early Warning Signs

When identifying past cases of genocide, many scholars work with some version of the typology of motives published in 1990 by historian Frank Chalk and sociologist Kurt Jonassohn in their book *The History and Sociology of Genocide*. The authors identify the following four motives and acknowledge that they may overlap, or several lesser motives might also drive a perpetrator:

1. To eliminate a real or potential threat, as in Imperial Rome's decision to annihilate Carthage in 146 BC.

2. To spread terror among real or potential enemies, as in Genghis Khan's destruction of city-states and people who rebelled against the Mongols in the thirteenth century.

3. To acquire economic wealth, as in the case of the Massachusetts Puritans' annihilation of the native Pequot people in 1637.

4. To implement a belief, theory, or an ideology, as in the case of Germany's decision under Hitler and the Nazis to destroy completely the Jewish people of Europe from 1941 to 1945.

Although these motives represent differing goals, they share common early warning signs of genocide. A good example of genocide in recent times that could have been prevented through close attention to early warning signs was the genocide of 1994 inflicted on the people labeled as "Tutsi" in Rwanda. Between 1959 and 1963, the predominantly Hutu political parties in power stigmatized all Tutsi as members of a hostile racial group, violently forcing their leaders and many civilians into exile in neighboring countries through a series of assassinations and massacres. Despite systematic exclusion of Tutsi from service in the military, government security agencies, and public service, as well as systematic discrimination against them in higher education, hundreds of thousands of Tutsi did remain behind in Rwanda. Government-issued cards identified each Rwandan as Hutu or Tutsi.

A generation later, some Tutsi raised in refugee camps in Uganda and elsewhere joined together, first organizing politically and then militarily, to reclaim a place in their homeland. When the predominantly Tutsi Rwanda Patriotic Front invaded Rwanda from Uganda in October 1990, extremist Hutu political parties demonized all of Rwanda's Tutsi as traitors, ratcheting up hate propaganda through radio broadcasts on government-run Radio Rwanda and privately owned radio station RTLM. Within the print media, *Kangura* and other publications used vicious cartoons to further demonize Tutsi and to stigmatize any Hutu who dared advocate bringing Tutsi into the government. Massacres of dozens and later hundreds of Tutsi sprang up even as Rwandans prepared to elect a coalition government led by moderate political parties, and as the United Nations dispatched a small international military force led by Canadian general Roméo Dallaire to oversee the elections and political transition. Late in 1992, an international human rights organization's investigating team detected the hate propaganda campaign, verified systematic massacres of Tutsi, and warned the international community that Rwanda had already entered the early stages of genocide, to no avail. On April 6, 1994, Rwanda's genocidal killing accelerated at an alarming pace when someone shot down the airplane flying Rwandan president Juvenal Habyarimana home from peace talks in Arusha, Tanzania.

Hundreds of thousands of Tutsi civilians—including children, women, and the elderly—died horrible deaths because the world ignored the early warning signs of the genocide and refused to act. Prominent among those early warning signs were: 1) systematic, government-decreed discrimination against the Tutsi as members of a supposed racial group; 2) government-issued identity cards labeling every Tutsi as a member of a racial group; 3) hate propaganda casting all Tutsi as subversives and traitors; 4) organized assassinations and massacres targeting Tutsi; and 5) indoctrination of militias and special military units to believe that all Tutsi posed a genocidal threat to the existence of Hutu and would enslave Hutu if they ever again became the rulers of Rwanda.

Genocide Prevention and the Responsibility to Protect

The shock waves emanating from the Rwanda genocide forced world leaders at least to acknowledge in principle that the national sovereignty of offending nations cannot trump the responsibility of those governments to prevent the infliction of mass atrocities on their own people. When governments violate that obligation, the member states of the United Nations have a responsibility to get involved. Such involvement can take the form of, first, offering to help the local government change its ways through technical advice and development aid, and second—if the local government persists in assaulting its own people—initiating armed intervention to protect the civilians at risk. In 2005 the United Nations began to implement the Responsibility to Protect initiative, a framework of principles to guide the international community in preventing mass atrocities.

As in many real-world domains, theory and practice often diverge. Genocide and crimes against humanity are rooted in problems that produce failing states: poverty, poor education, extreme nationalism, lawlessness, dictatorship, and corruption. Implementing the principles of the Responsibility to Protect doctrine burdens intervening state leaders with the necessity of addressing each of those problems over a long period of time. And when those problems prove too intractable and complex to solve easily, the citizens of the intervening nations may lose patience, voting out the leader who initiated the intervention. Arguments based solely on humanitarian principles fail to overcome such concerns. What is needed to persuade political leaders to stop preventable mass atrocities are compelling arguments based on their own national interests.

Preventable mass atrocities threaten the national interests of all states in five specific ways:

1. Mass atrocities create conditions that engender widespread and concrete threats from terrorism, piracy, and other forms of lawlessness on the land and sea;
2. Mass atrocities facilitate the spread of warlordism, whose tentacles block affordable access to vital raw materials produced in the affected country and threaten the prosperity of all nations that depend on the consumption of these resources;
3. Mass atrocities trigger cascades of refugees and internally displaced populations that, combined with climate change and growing international air travel, will accelerate the worldwide incidence of lethal infectious diseases;

4. Mass atrocities spawn single-interest parties and political agendas that drown out more diverse political discourse in the countries where the atrocities take place and in the countries that host large numbers of refugees. Xenophobia and nationalist backlashes are the predictable consequences of government indifference to mass atrocities elsewhere that could have been prevented through early actions;

5. Mass atrocities foster the spread of national and transnational criminal networks trafficking in drugs, women, arms, contraband, and laundered money.

Alerting elected political representatives to the consequences of mass atrocities should be part of every student movement's agenda in the twenty-first century. Adam Smith, the great political economist and author of *The Wealth of Nations*, put it best when he wrote: "It is not from the benevolence of the butcher, the brewer, or the baker that we expect our dinner, but from their regard to their own interest." Self-interest is a powerful engine for good in the marketplace and can be an equally powerful motive and source of inspiration for state action to prevent genocide and mass persecution. In today's new global village, the lives we save may be our own.

Frank Chalk

Frank Chalk, who has a doctorate from the University of Wisconsin-Madison, is a professor of history and director of the Montreal Institute for Genocide and Human Rights Studies at Concordia University in Montreal, Canada. He is coauthor, with Kurt

Jonassohn, of The History and Sociology of Genocide *(1990); coauthor, with General Roméo Dallaire, Kyle Matthews, Carla Barqueiro, and Simon Doyle, of* Mobilizing the Will to Intervene: Leadership to Prevent Mass Atrocities *(2010); and associate editor of the three-volume Macmillan Reference USA* Encyclopedia of Genocide and Crimes Against Humanity *(2004). Chalk served as president of the International Association of Genocide Scholars from June 1999 to June 2001. His current research focuses on the use of radio and television broadcasting in the incitement and prevention of genocide, and domestic laws on genocide. For more information on genocide and examples of the experiences of people displaced by genocide and other human rights violations, interested readers can consult the websites of the Montreal Institute for Genocide and Human Rights Studies (http://migs.concordia.ca) and the Montreal Life Stories project (www.lifestoriesmontreal.ca).*

World Map

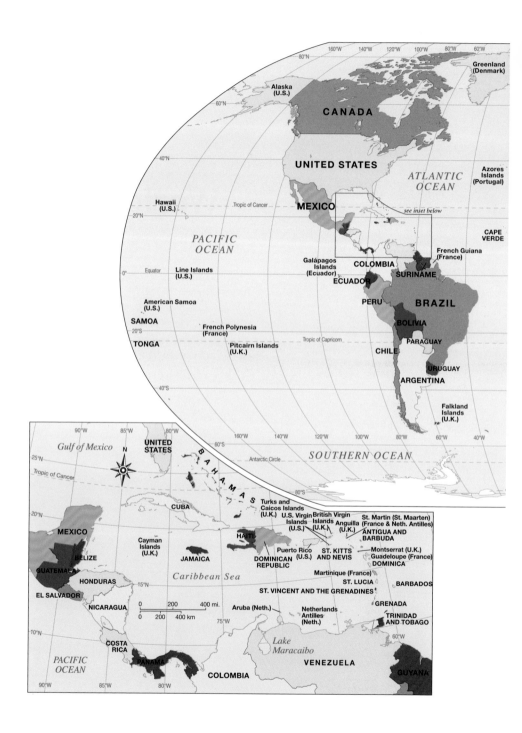

160°W 140°W 120°W 100°W 80°W 60°W

80°N

Greenland
(Denmark)

Alaska
(U.S.)

60°N

CANADA

40°N

UNITED STATES

*ATLANTIC
OCEAN*

Azores
Islands
(Portugal)

Hawaii
(U.S.)

Tropic of Cancer

MEXICO

see inset below

20°N

CAPE
VERDE

*PACIFIC
OCEAN*

0° Equator Line Islands
(U.S.)

Galápagos
Islands
(Ecuador)

COLOMBIA

French Guiana
(France)

SURINAME

ECUADOR

American Samoa
(U.S.)

PERU

BRAZIL

SAMOA

BOLIVIA

20°S

French Polynesia
(France)

PARAGUAY

TONGA

Pitcairn Islands
(U.K.)

Tropic of Capricorn

CHILE

URUGUAY

40°S

ARGENTINA

Falkland
Islands
(U.K.)

90°W 85°W 80°W

Gulf of Mexico

**UNITED
STATES**

N

160°W 140°W 120°W 100°W 80°W 60°W 40°W

60°S

B
A
H
A
M
A
S

SOUTHERN OCEAN

25°N

Tropic of Cancer

Antarctic Circle

CUBA

Turks and
Caicos Islands
(U.K.)

80°S

20°N

U.S. Virgin British Virgin
Islands Islands Anguilla
(U.S.) (U.K.) (U.K.)

St. Martin (St. Maarten)
(France & Neth. Antilles)

MEXICO

Cayman
Islands
(U.K.)

HAITI

**ANTIGUA AND
BARBUDA**

BELIZE

JAMAICA

Puerto Rico
(U.S.)

**DOMINICAN
REPUBLIC**

**ST. KITTS
AND NEVIS**

Montserrat (U.K.)
Guadeloupe (France)

GUATEMALA

DOMINICA

Caribbean Sea

Martinique (France)

HONDURAS

ST. LUCIA

BARBADOS

EL SALVADOR

ST. VINCENT AND THE GRENADINES

NICARAGUA

0 200 400 mi.

GRENADA

0 200 400 km

75°W

Aruba (Neth.)

Netherlands
Antilles
(Neth.)

**TRINIDAD
AND TOBAGO**

60°W

*PACIFIC
OCEAN*

**COSTA
RICA**

PANAMA

*Lake
Maracaibo*

VENEZUELA

GUYANA

90°W 85°W 80°W

COLOMBIA

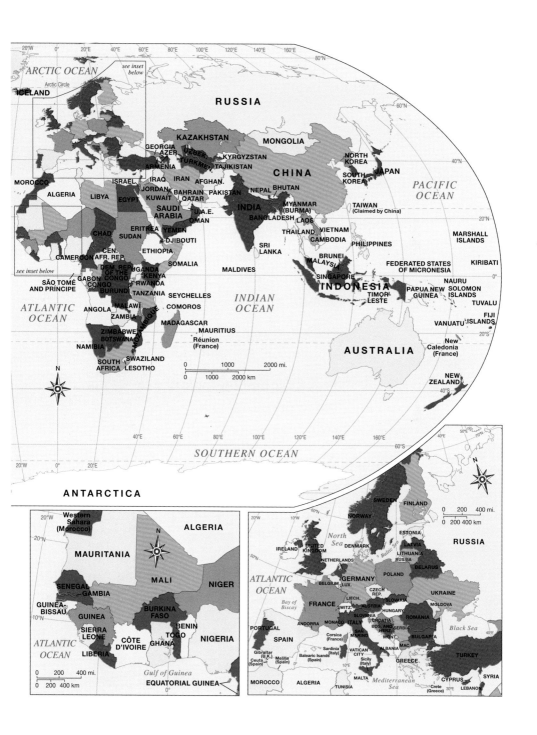

Chronology

1815	African American sailor Paul Cuffee establishes the first African American settlement in Sierra Leone.
July 1847	Liberia declares independence from the United States.
1936	Forced labor in Liberia is abolished.
1944	William V.S. Tubman is elected to the Liberian presidency and serves seven terms.
1971	Tubman dies in office; William Tolbert Jr. replaces him as president.
April 14, 1979	Protests against the increased cost of rice end in riots. The Liberian army fires on civilians, killing more than forty people.
1980	A coup overthrows Tolbert, who is killed. Master Sergeant Samuel K. Doe becomes the head of Liberia.
1989	The National Patriotic Front of Liberia (NPFL), led by Charles Taylor, begins a rebellion against Doe's government. This is the start of the first Liberian Civil War.
1990	Doe is executed by rebel forces.
	The Economic Community of West African States (ECOWAS) sends peace-keeping forces into Liberia.

1995	ECOWAS brokers a cease-fire between the warring factions. After a brief lull, violence starts again.
1996	The first Liberian Civil War ends.
1997	Taylor is elected president.
1999	Taylor's support for Revolutionary United Front rebels in Sierra Leone causes tension with Ghana, Nigeria, and Guinea. Rebel uprisings occur in northern Liberia. This is the start of the second Liberian Civil War.
July 2003	Taylor is indicted for war crimes because of his backing of Sierra Leone rebels.
August 2003	After intense fighting in Monrovia and the arrival of ECOWAS peacekeepers, Taylor leaves Liberia. US troops arrive and a peace treaty is signed. This is the end of the second Liberian Civil War.
November 23, 2005	Ellen Johnson Sirleaf is elected as president of Liberia.
February 2006	The Liberian Truth and Reconciliation Commission (TRC) is established to investigate human rights abuses in the country between 1979 and 2003.
June 2006	The International Criminal Court (ICC) in the Netherlands agrees to hear Taylor's trial on charges of crimes against humanity.
June 2009	The TRC releases its final report. Sirleaf, who initially supported Taylor,

is included in a list of forty-nine people who the TRC says should be barred from public office.

January 2011 The Supreme Court of Liberia rules that the TRC recommendations to bar individuals from public office are not constitutionally binding because the accused received no due process.

November 2011 Sirleaf is elected to a second term as president.

April 26, 2012 The ICC rules that Taylor is guilty of crimes against humanity.

September 27, 2013 Taylor's conviction is confirmed on appeal. He prepares to be transferred to a British prison to serve a fifty-year prison sentence.

CHAPTER 1

Historical Background on Liberia

Chapter Exercises

STATISTICS

	Liberia
Total Area	111,369 sq km World ranking: 104
Population	3,989,703 (July 2013 estimate) World ranking: 127
Ethnic Groups	Kpelle 20.3%, Bassa 13.4%, Grebo 10%, Gio 8%, Mano 7.9%, Kru 6%, Lorma 5.1%, Kissi 4.8%, Gola 4.4%, other 20.1% (2008 census)
Religions	Christian 85.6%, Muslim 12.2%, Traditional 0.6%, other 0.2%, none 1.4% (2008 census)
Literacy (total population)	60.8%
GDP	$2.719 billion (2012 estimate) World ranking: 3185

Source: *The World Factbook*. Washington, DC: Central Intelligence Agency, 2013. www.cia.gov.

1. Analyzing Statistics

Question 1: Is there a majority ethnicity in Liberia? What aspects of Liberia's ethnic makeup contributed to a complicated relationship between ethnicity and violence?

Question 2: What is the majority religious group in Liberia? What aspects of Liberia's history account for this? Does there appear to be a link between ethnicity and religion?

Question 3: Given Liberia's world rank in GDP, is it a poor country or a rich one? What role did Liberia's economic status play in sparking violence?

2. Writing Prompt

Write an article describing the violence and atrocities committed by Samuel K. Doe's regime. Begin the article with a strong title that will captivate the audience. Include any appropriate background information the reader may need to better understand the events. Give details about the events that answer who, what, when, where, and why.

3. Group Activity

In small groups, discuss the role of the diamond trade in fueling violence in Liberia and West Africa. Compose a speech making a recommendation on what actions the international community should take regarding the diamond trade.

Overview of the Liberian Civil Wars

Daniel Elwood Dunn

Daniel Elwood Dunn is professor emeritus of political science at the University of the South in Sewanee, Tennessee. In the following viewpoint, he traces the history of Liberia from its colonization by African Americans through the more than twenty years of violence that began with the overthrow of William Tolbert Jr. in 1980. Dunn points to numerous causes of the violence, including resentment toward descendants of African American colonists, ethnic tensions, a struggle over the control of diamond resources, and the actions of individual leaders.

The beginnings of Liberia as a modern state are rooted in American circumstances that led to a back-to-Africa movement among a relatively small number of African-Americans, and which was supported by white American sponsors. With multiple motives, some far from charitable, the American Colonization Society launched the Liberian experiment in the early years of the nineteenth century. Liberia's initial purpose was to serve as a beachhead for the redemption of Africa from

Daniel Elwood Dunn, "Liberia," *Encyclopedia of Genocide and Crimes Against Humanity,* Macmillan Reference USA, 2005, pp. 648–653. From *Encyclopedia of Genocide and Crimes Against Humanity*, 1E. Copyright © 2005 by Cengage Learning. All rights reserved. Reproduced with permission.

its perceived state of degradation. The agencies of this redeeming work were to be, in order of importance, the white man, the westernized black man, and then at the bottom of the heap, the non-westernized African peoples. Much of what became public policy in early Liberia rested on this hierarchical vision of human civilization. Liberia labored under this vision through the rest of the nineteenth century and into the early decades of the twentieth century.

The Rise of President Doe

A paradigm shift occurred at the end of World War II, when Liberia's supporters and its citizens moved from a commitment to their founding mission of civilizing and Christianizing the peoples of Africa and adopted in its place a philosophy of natural rights and its offshoot of democratic governance and respect for fundamental human rights. In a real sense Liberia was in the throes of this shift when the coup d'état of 1980 occurred.

Immediately prior to the coup, during the administration of President William R. Tolbert (1971–1980), a national reform movement was initiated. Tolbert had clear reformist proclivities, but he was not a strong political leader. Challenging Tolbert were several politically progressive groups, notably the Progressive Alliance of Liberia (PAL) and the Movement for Justice in Africa (MOJA). They were perceived as legitimate alternatives to the regime then in power.

There were many confrontations between advocates of change and those who wished to preserve the status quo before the fateful challenge occurred. Then the government announced the possibility of an increase in the price of rice, the country's staple food. The PAL demanded that the price of rice be left unchanged and signaled that, unless the government acceded to its demands, it would call for a mass rally to press its case. When the government replied that the price increase was only under discussion, and refused to grant PAL the necessary demonstration permit, PAL defiantly called for the rally anyway.

An unprecedented clash ensued between a throng of demonstrators and the government's security forces on April 14, 1979. Many of the demonstrators were killed, scores were maimed, and millions of dollars worth of property was destroyed or damaged. The demonstrators were expressing widespread disgust and anger with the entire political system, and voiced their dissatisfaction with the president, who symbolized that system.

The government attempted to put down the dissidents, but its efforts failed because the society was perilously divided, especially within the nation's security forces. The police were prepared to carry out government orders, but military personnel refused to fire into the demonstrators, pointing out that their own children and kinsmen might be in the crowd. Abandoned and insecure, the Tolbert administration sought and received military assistance from President Sekou Touré of Guinea. When Guinean military forces arrived in Liberia, the Liberian military and a great many Liberian civilians were deeply offended.

On April 12, 1980, seventeen enlisted men in the Liberian Army led an attack on the President's mansion under the leadership of Master Sergeant Samuel K. Doe. They assassinated President Tolbert and overthrew his government, creating a new governing body, the People's Redemption Council (PRC), and Doe assumed the interim presidency.

The coupmakers' declaration of intent upon seizing power convinced most observers that the new government would implement progressive policies. They released all political prisoners and invited key figures in the opposition to help them form a new government. A progressive political agenda was announced, and it appeared that Doe and his followers were about to impose significant changes on the country by fiat. Accompanying the expression of intent, however, was a pattern of behavior that belied the stated progressive aims. Military personnel and other regime figures quickly adopted opulent lifestyles, lording it over their subordinates. More ominous still, the new regime began singling out individuals and families that they deemed associates of the deposed Tolbert administration. This development became clearer when, in the weeks following the coup, the PRC suddenly and publicly executed thirteen senior officials of the old regime. The executions touched off an international chorus of outrage and condemnation for this gross violation of rights, as did the apparent targeting of dissident Liberians for execution or persecution.

Regardless of internal and international outcries, these persecutions and secret executions continued. Soon, deadly conflicts sprang up within the PRC itself, as personality differences led to political purges. Several senior PRC members were executed on President Doe's orders. Eventually, Doe found himself in conflict with Commanding General Thomas Quiwonkpa, a popular soldier and a senior member of the PRC. After several bloody encounters between the Doe and Quiwonkpa factions, Quiwonkpa was forced to flee the country.

Fall of the Doe Regime

In 1985 two major events transpired. The first was a purported democratic election. When the people voted against Doe's military regime, the government illegally intervened in the process and reversed the outcome, declaring Doe the winner. The second event was Quiwonkpa's reappearance in Monrovia on November 12, 1985. Upon his return to Liberia, he attempted to lead a coup against Doe and install the candidate who was popularly believed to have won the election. Quiwonkpa's coup attempt failed. Incensed, President Doe carried out a rash of retaliatory killings. Estimates as to the number executed during this period range from 500 to as many as 3,000. The victims were largely drawn from the police, military, and security personnel of Nimba county, which was the home region of Quiwonkpa. The many who were killed were buried in mass graves in Nimba.

The Western media soon created a shorthand for understanding the gathering conflict, blaming the violence as arising from an ethnicity-based conflict between the Krahn (Doe's

A woman asks for help in front of the US Embassy in Monrovia, Liberia, in July 2003. Bodies were placed near the embassy to protest the United States' delay in sending peacekeeping troops. © Chris Hondros/Getty Images.

people) and his Mandingo supporters versus the Dhan and Mano peoples of Nimba County. This was only partially true, however. Doe was in fact lashing out at all opponents, real and imagined, regardless of their ethnic background. As a result, his presidency devolved into a reign of terror.

Doe was inaugurated President of Liberia in January 1986. He soon found it difficult to rule, however. The violence that followed the elections, coupled, in a curious way, with the events that immediately followed his own coup of 1980, engendered covert protests that eventually became open acts of rebellion. By the start of 1989, Liberia became increasingly unsafe.

A fallout in Africa at the end of the Cold War was the emergence of the warlord insurgencies threatening to destabilize national governments. On Christmas Eve of 1989, the insurgent leader, Charles Taylor, announced to the Liberian and international media that he was heading an insurgency under the banner of the National Patriotic Front of Liberia (NPFL). His goal was to bring down the Doe regime and end the reign of terror. He set himself the goal of completing the unfinished work of Thomas Quiwonkpa.

Civil War Erupts

Taylor's rebels advanced from the border between Liberia and neighboring Ivory Coast. As they penetrated Nimba County, Doe responded by initiating a scorched earth policy, sending his soldiers to raze whole villages and kill everything that moved. This tactic quickly galvanized the people, first in Nimba County, then in the nation as a whole. As the insurgency gathered momentum, the brutality on both sides was unparalleled in the history of Liberia. The violence was not limited to a clash between armies; tens of thousands of civilians died, and countless others were maimed or otherwise injured by the war.

The extreme violence early in the civil war was a consequence of problems at three levels. First was the inter-ethnic hostility that existed between Doe's Krahn and Mandingo supporters and the remnants of Quiwonkpa's Dahn and Mano followers, who now rallied behind Charles Taylor. Second, the Liberian population was, and is, comprised of a great many other ethnicities, distinguished by language and culture, so no true sense of shared national identity could be called upon to mitigate the violence. Finally, Liberia suffered from international neglect after the Cold War ended and Africa ceased to be viewed as strategically important to the United States, its traditional ally. The result for the Liberian people was that more than 200,000 of Liberia's 2.6 million people were killed, another 800,000 became internally displaced persons, and more than 700,000 fled abroad to live as refugees.

As the rebel groups approached Monrovia in early 1990 and engaged Doe's Armed Forces of Liberia (AFL), the slaughter increased. Some 2,000 Dhan and Mano, mostly women and children, sought refuge at the International Red Cross station in the main Lutheran Church compound in Monrovia. Although the Red Cross insignia were clearly visible, AFL death squads invaded the refuge on the night of July 29, 1990, and massacred the more than 600 people who sheltered there. In the days that followed, the death squads roamed the streets of Monrovia and its environs, attacking any civilians suspected of being sympathetic to the rebels or lukewarm toward Doe's regime.

By mid-1990 Doe's control of the country was limited to the area around the presidential palace. Prince Johnson, leader of the breakaway Independent National Patriotic Front of Liberia (INPF), risked a meeting with Doe at the Barclay Training Center (a military barracks) in Monrovia on August 18, 1990. Doe suggested that Johnson join him in a "native solidarity" alliance against Taylor, who was accused of representing "settler" interests (meaning the interests of descendants of the African Americans who came to the region in the nineteenth century). Johnson declined the offer of alliance and returned to his base on the outskirts of Monrovia.

A few days after this meeting, Doe led a foray into terri-tory held by Johnson's forces in order to visit the leaders of the Economic Community Monitoring Group (ECOMOG), a peace-keeping force that the economic community of West African states (ECOWAS) has created in an effort to help resolve African conflicts. During this foray, however, Doe's entourage was at-tacked, most were killed, and Doe himself was captured. Badly injured and bleeding from serious leg wounds, he was taken to Prince Johnson's compound. There he was tortured and then left to bleed to death, the whole gruesome episode captured by Johnson's video camera. On September 10, 1990, he died and his naked body was placed on public display.

Taylor's Rise to Power

With Doe's death, the struggle for power intensified. The rival factions headed by Taylor and Johnson now faced a third chal-lenger: a civilian Interim Government of National Unity (IGNU). This entity was the creation of an ECOWAS-sponsored summit meeting held in Gambia, where the leaders of Liberia's neighbors in West Africa sought ways to end the conflict. Professor Amos Sawyer, a Liberian national, was chosen the head of the IGNU by a representative body of Liberian political and civil leaders.

Two years later, the conflict still raged on. Taylor attempted to seize Monrovia, in October 1992. His self-styled "Operation Octopus" was a bloody military showdown in which he pitted an army of children (their ages ranged from 8 to 15) against the pro-fessional soldiers of ECOMOG. Thousands were slain, including five American nuns serving homeless Liberian children. Taylor's coup attempt failed.

By 1996 a coalition government composed of former rebel leaders and civilians had been put in place, but endemic dis-trust led to a second showdown in Monrovia. Three members of the ruling Council of State, Charles Taylor of the NPFL, Alhaji Kromah of the United Liberation Movement of Liberia, and Wilton Sankawolo, the civilian chair of the Council, attempted to arrest another government minister, Roosevelt Johnson, for allegations of murder. Seven weeks of fighting ensued and, once again, thousands of Liberians—mostly civilians—were killed. This phase of the civil war ended when regional and international peace facilitators decided to hold new elections, in which warlords were permitted to participate. Taylor, according to some observers, won the vote, but other election observers have suggested that many who voted for him did so only out of fear. Taylor promised peace, but he was unable to establish legitimacy for his presidency at either the domestic or international level.

The Conflict in Sierra Leone

In fact, just as Liberia appeared to be settling down, neighboring Sierra Leone erupted into war, with the May 25, 1997, overthrow of that country's elected government. Taylor had undergone guerrilla insurgency training in Libya in the late 1980s alongside Foday Sankoh and other West African dissidents. An informal pact was made between Taylor and Sankoh that they would remain in solidarity as they embarked upon violently changing the political order in the subregion. Sankoh fought with Taylor's NPFL, and when in 1991 Sankoh's RUF appeared on the Sierra Leone scene, a close relationship characterized their leaders. Thus, when the 1997 coup brought Sankoh's Revolutionary United Front (RUF) into power, however briefly, Taylor was prepared to recognize Sankoh's claim to legitimacy and assist his Sierra Leonian ally.

The destabilizing effects of Taylor's support of the RUF were not only felt in Sierra Leone, but throughout much of West Africa. This led the United Nations to order an investigation. The resulting UN Security Council Panel of Experts Report implicated the President of Liberia in the exploitation of Sierra Leone's diamond mines through his ties with the RUF, and of using a portion of the proceeds to keep the RUF supplied with arms. The charges were clearly documented, but Taylor stoutly denied them. Despite his denials, in May 2001 the UN Security Council imposed punitive sanctions on Liberia.

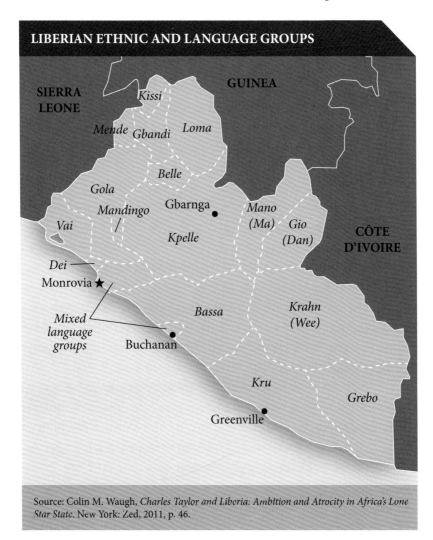

LIBERIAN ETHNIC AND LANGUAGE GROUPS

SIERRA LEONE

Kissi

GUINEA

Mende Gbandi Loma

Belle

Gola

Mandingo Gbarnga

Mano (Ma) Gio (Dan)

CÔTE D'IVOIRE

Vai

Kpelle

Dei

Monrovia ★

Mixed language groups

Buchanan

Bassa

Krahn (Wee)

Kru

Grebo

Greenville

Source: Colin M. Waugh, *Charles Taylor and Liberia: Ambition and Atrocity in Africa's Lone Star State.* New York: Zed, 2011, p. 46.

The End of Taylor's Regime

In 2002 the war in Sierra Leone was largely contained, due to massive international intervention, and democratic elections were held. Sankoh's RUF, now transformed into the Revolutionary United Party (RUP), was roundly defeated. For his part in supporting the RUF, Taylor's government in Liberia was now internationally viewed as a pariah regime. Taylor's troubles, however, had begun three years earlier, when a group of Liberians formed a rebel group called Liberians United For Reconciliation and Democracy (LURD). LURD's stated objective was Taylor's removal from power because of his atrocious human rights record and the impunity that generally characterized his leadership.

LURD stepped up its attacks in early 2003, and a new rebel group, the Movement for Democracy in Liberia (MODEL), made its appearance in March. MODEL quickly gained ascendancy in the southern part of the country, whereas LURD's power was concentrated in the north. In March, LURD's forces opened several fronts, advancing to within a few miles of Monrovia. Tens of thousands of civilians were displaced during the fighting. On June 4 of the same year, Taylor was indicted by the UN sponsored Special Court in Sierra Leone for his complicity in war crimes and crimes against humanity arising from his activities in that country. U.S. President George W. Bush publicly called on Taylor to resign and leave the country, thus increasing the pressure on Taylor's regime.

On July 17, a LURD offensive into the capital resulted in hundreds more killed and displaced persons. International intervention finally produced a respite, as international facilitators set up peace talks in Ghana. Taylor bowed to the pressures on August 11, when he handed power over to his vice president and accepted exile in Nigeria. The peace talks concluded on August 18, and on August 21 a new leader, Gyude Bryant, was chosen to chair an interim government. To maintain the peace, the UN Security Council sent 15,000 peacekeeping troops and set up a rescue operation to help deal with the aftermath of two decades of bloody civil wars.

Samuel K. Doe's Regime Struggles to Rule Liberia After the Assassination of Tolbert

Gregory Jaynes

Gregory Jaynes has been a correspondent for Time, Life, *and the* New York Times. *In the following viewpoint, he describes the early chaotic days of the Samuel K. Doe administration, which overthrew President William Tolbert Jr. in a coup in 1980. Jaynes reports that Doe, a master sergeant, has little grasp of economic policy. He also notes that the government under Doe has issued dictatorial orders. However, he writes that some observers have expressed hope that Doe's government is learning and that it may be willing to pass over power to civilian control once the country is stabilized.*

It has been nine months [as of January 1981] since 17 noncommissioned officers in the Liberian Army rose up from their tumbledown, tin-on-tin barracks on a beach below the Executive Mansion here, shot and bayoneted President William R. Tolbert Jr., and took over the Government without half a notion of how to run a country.

"If it weren't for the bloodshed and the enormous economic problems," Amos Dawson, the dean of Liberia College, said the other day, "you could characterize a lot of what has happened as

Gregory Jaynes, "Liberia's Young Sergeant Still Learning How to Rule," *New York Times,* January 20, 1981. Reproduced with permission.

amusing." Moreover, said a high civilian official in the new revolutionary Government, "to cope, you have to regard a lot of what goes on as comedic."

An Unprepared Chief Executive

The man who became Liberia's leader after the coup, the 20th head of state this country has had since it was founded by freed American slaves in 1847, is Master Sgt. Samuel Kanyon Doe, an 11th-grade dropout who was trained two years ago by a United States special forces unit.

He became Liberia's chief executive on April 12, 1980, not because he aspired to the job, but merely because he was the ranking officer involved in Mr. Tolbert's assassination. Master Sergeant Doe, [six] lower ranking sergeants, eight corporals and two privates became the Government of Liberia, known as the People's Redemption Council.

The soldiers gave as their reasons for the coup more than a century of domination by the descendants of the freed American slaves who set up Africa's oldest republic, corruption by the Tolbert Government and economic deprivation of the 1.8 million Liberians at the hands of the 90,000 "Americo-Liberians."

Sergeant Doe increased the pay of the lowest ranking soldiers from $75 to $250 a month and also gave raises to higher paid officers and to civil servants. He promised to hold down the price of gasoline and rice, a staple. Almost a year to the day before the coup, there had been bloody riots here over an increase in the price of rice.

The 28-year-old, modest new head of state eschewed his predecessor's West German limousine, first in favor of a Chevrolet and later a Honda Civic. His illiterate wife, Nancy, the mother of his two children, started bringing home-cooked, hot lunches to his office.

Learning to Govern

The learning process began. First the soldiers, most of them in their 20's, learned that the Government had $5 million in the central bank and that it owed $700 million in foreign debts. A former Finance Minister under President Tolbert, an adviser to the revolutionary Government before leaving to live in the United States, endeavored to explain delicately to the sergeant that he had to raise the price of gasoline.

Initially, Sergeant Doe held to his promise to freeze prices. Exasperated, the financial adviser finally blurted, "You don't sign this paper, country go blooey." The sergeant signed. Gasoline prices have doubled, to $2.80 a gallon.

For a while it seemed to Liberia's educated elite that the country was being run by the "Keystone Kops." The head of state threatened the national soccer team with imprisonment if it did not win a match with Gambia. The match ended in a tie.

About 700 civil servants were jailed, but most were freed within a few days and charged $8.50 for each day of their incarceration, $3.50 for a light bulb and $5 for water.

Corporals used their guns instead of their tongues to resolve arguments. A vast though undisclosed number of skilled Liberians emigrated.

The military took over many of Monrovia's fancy houses. They took the screens off the windows of the house that had belonged to former Foreign Minister Charles Cecil Dennis Jr., who had been executed. The next-door neighbor asked why. "To let the chickens in, of course," a corporal said.

The People's Redemption Council wrecked so many cars that it had to impose a rule on itself: Wreck one and the Government buys you a replacement; wreck two and you buy your own.

Ever so slowly, though, the Redemption Council appears to be learning how to govern. "They have learned what they don't know," said a bank manager who asked that his name and his nationality not be disclosed. Diplomats say that Sergeant Doe has become much more aware of his responsibilities, that he is asserting himself more and that he has cut back the instances in which soldiers get out of line.

People celebrate in the streets of Monrovia, Liberia, after the overthrow of President William Tolbert on April 12, 1980. © Bettmann/Corbis.

Moreover, Western diplomats say, the sergeant himself at last has a grasp of how tenuous Liberia's economy is, though not much of an idea of how to stabilize it beyond seeking loans.

Dealing with a Shortfall in Revenues

The country's monthly revenue, mostly from iron ore and rubber, is about $17 million. Its monthly expenditures are about $30 million, including $7 million in debt repayments. Last month, Liberia barely avoided bankruptcy with a hastily assembled American emergency grant of $7 million. This month, four foreign banks managed to put together a $4 million loan to get the Government over the hump. An official in the American Embassy here calls it putting Band-Aids on hemorrhages.

To his credit, Sergeant Doe has taken some steps that have brought him a degree of confidence from international bankers. He has told Government agencies that they cannot ask for another dime for the time being. Announcing that "our policy shall be to repair rather than to replace," he has stopped the purchase of any new equipment.

He has also frozen Government hiring. This month the Government will start taking deductions for mandatory national savings bonds from all salaried employees. The bonds are expected to raise a quick $50 million. They are to be paid back to the employees, with interest, in five years. The policies helped persuade the International Monetary Fund to provide Liberia with $85 million toward this year's budget of $372.5 million.

Sergeant Doe reportedly says that he would like nothing better than to return Liberia to civilian rule, but that he wants to pull the country out of its economic mess first. Civilians capable of running a government say they are not all that anxious to assume the headaches now anyway. And before the army can return to the barracks, they must have new barracks. Conditions in the present ones had a great deal to do with the killing of President Tolbert.

"I want you to talk to the master sergeant," George Boley, executive assistant to the head of state, said to an American correspondent recently. "I want you to see we are not nincompoops. And I want you to see the barracks. The reason the soldiers are in town is they don't want to be in the barracks. No water at all or muddy water. Their children have diarrhea all the time."

As it turned out, Sergeant Doe had a cold. When a journalist got into his office, tape recorder in hand, the sergeant said: "Cut the tape. Cut it." Then he explained that he would like to chat for two hours, but felt too ill to talk for one minute. The interview was over.

The Diamond Trade Fuels Violence in Liberia and Surrounding Countries

Lansana Gberie

Lansana Gberie is senior researcher at the Africa Conflict Prevention Programme of the Institute for Security Studies (ISS) in Addis Ababa, Ethiopia, and the editor of Rescuing a Fragile State: Sierra Leone 2002–2008. *In the following viewpoint, he argues that fighters in Liberia and countries around it waged war for control of resources. Smuggling of timber and diamonds enriched warlords such as Charles Taylor and funded further conflict. According to Gberie, international willingness to deal in smuggled goods essentially enabled and encouraged the terrible violence in Liberia, Sierra Leone, Ghana, Côte d'Ivoire, and Guinea.*

> It is not just about Sierra Leone, it is regional and international, and in some instances it is worldwide. And it boils down to diamonds.
>
> *David Crane, Chief Prosecutor, Special Court for*
> *Sierra Leone, 2003*

Unlike Southern Africa, where diamond discoveries since the 1860s helped to shape the destiny of the entire region

Lansana Gberie, "West Africa: Rocks in a Hard Place: The Political Economy of Diamonds and Regional Destabilization," The Diamonds and Human Society Project, Occasional Paper #9, 2003, pp. 1–4. Reproduced with permission.

south of the Limpopo, diamonds only became a factor in West Africa in the mid 20th century. Ghana (then British-ruled Gold Coast) was the first to register significant commercial exploitation of diamonds in the region, beginning in 1919. The next significant discoveries were in Sierra Leone, over ten years later, in 1930. Commercial exploitation started in 1935, soon surpassing the Ghanaian industry in value, and in both social and political significance. Guinean diamonds were discovered two years after Sierra Leone's, in 1932, but significant commercial exploitation, hampered by low returns and the advent of World War II, began only in the 1950s, and did not became a serious factor in the country's political and economic development until recent years. Liberia's diamond industry is smaller and far less organized than its neighbours, and although production, beginning in the 1950s, peaked at 150,000 carats per annum for several years in the 1970s, they were mainly small industrial stones. Throughout the years, Liberia has been important where diamonds are concerned, mainly because it was a fencing nation for high quality diamonds smuggled from Sierra Leone. Côte d'Ivoire's diamond industry, the least important in the region, was a low-level affair, under well-regulated corporate control from the 1960s to the early 1980s when the diamond deposits appeared to have been exhausted. Today, the industry is left mainly to informal miners, and official control is minimal. The main diamond areas, around Korhogo in the north of country, came under rebel control at the end of 2002. The other two countries of interest in the region, Burkina Faso and Gambia, have no known diamond reserves but have been shady players in the region's illegal diamond trade. Indeed, Burkina Faso, became a very important player in Africa's conflict diamond nexus.

Criminality and Violence

In the 1960s, West African diamond production, at 7.5 million carats per annum, represented 26 per cent of global output. But by 1983, while over-all global production increased to around

40 million carats, West African production had fallen below one million carats a year. There were several reasons for this, ranging from the exhaustion or near-exhaustion of reserves (Côte d'Ivoire in particular) to the collapse of governmental control and the rampant smuggling and other irregularities which accompanied it. The decline of Sierra Leone's diamond industry, which was in the 1960s and 1970s the region's largest, with exports peaking at two million carats a year, illustrates the problem. Under the incompetent rule of President Joseph Momoh (1985–1991), almost all economic activities in Sierra Leone, already in long-term decline since the days of Momoh's despotic and corrupt pre-decessor Siaka Stevens, became terminally sclerotic. During the 1980s, two groups of players competed to milk the country's diamond reserves: a community of expatriate and settler Lebanese (who had dominated the informal industry from the beginning) and elements of a Russian/Israeli mafia. Among others, Russian mobsters Shaptai Kalmanovitch and Marat Balagula financed both licit and illicit mining, smuggling gems to Thailand, where they were reportedly swapped for heroin, which was then distributed in Europe. In 1988, official diamond exports had fallen to only 50,000 carats.

While this level of criminality was intolerable, the 1990s brought a much more toxic connection to the illegal diamond trade. Sierra Leone's decade-long war, beginning in 1991 and officially ending in January, 2002, provides the classic case of a diamond-fuelled war. But the story of resource-driven warfare begins earlier, in neighbouring Liberia. Its spread to Sierra Leone and then Guinea can only be understood in the context of the warlord political economy that developed in Liberia. On Christmas Eve 1989, a fugitive former Liberian official named Charles Gbankay Taylor led a group of about 150 armed fighters in an attack on Liberia from a base in Côte d'Ivoire. The ostensible reason was to overthrow the bloodthirsty dictatorship of President (formerly Master Sergeant) Samuel K. Doe, but the campaign soon after devolved into ethnic massacres and banditry. At first, Taylor sponsored his war by looting Liberia's rich hardwood timber reserves, reportedly making hundreds of millions of dollars for himself in the process. Diamonds played little, if any, role in Taylor's Liberian campaigns, partly because Liberia's diamond mines were already in shambles by the time he struck. But Taylor learned during his campaigns that he could operate with relative freedom in his illegal exploitation of the country's rich extractive resources, finding ready buyers from Europe and elsewhere, and safe conduits and havens in Côte d'Ivoire and Burkina Faso.

When Taylor's ambition to capture Monrovia was frustrated in 1990 by the intervention of troops from the Economic Community of West African States (ECOWAS)—the intervention force was called ECOMOG—he consolidated his hold on the parts of the country he had overrun, which he called 'Greater Liberia', creating what William Reno has called the quintessential 'warlord economy.' Tens of millions of dollars worth of timber was shipped from 'Greater Liberia', mainly to France and Italy through the Ivorian port town of San Pedro. It was not so much that the conflict created, to quote two scholars who have studied the phenomenon of private economic activity in armed conflict, a 'niche market for companies willing to avoid regulation and assume greater levels of risk.' It was that companies and governments, in Europe and Africa, actively colluded in the looting of Liberia for short-term gains and for dubious political reasons. When Sierra Leone's diamonds entered the fray, the number of players multiplied, and the stakes became much higher.

Sierra Leone's Diamond-Fueled War

During the stalemate occasioned by the West African ECO-MOG peacekeeping intervention, Taylor mentored, trained and armed Sierra Leone's Revolutionary United Front (RUF), which launched its first attacks against border towns in Sierra Leone in March 1991. Taylor provided the RUF with the same kind of safe haven provided to him by Côte d'Ivoire and Burkina Faso,

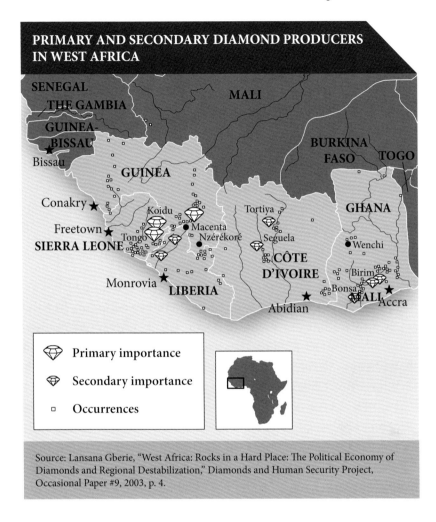

PRIMARY AND SECONDARY DIAMOND PRODUCERS IN WEST AFRICA

Primary importance

Secondary importance

□ Occurrences

Source: Lansana Gberie, "West Africa: Rocks in a Hard Place: The Political Economy of Diamonds and Regional Destabilization," Diamonds and Human Security Project, Occasional Paper #9, 2003, p. 4.

and when the RUF captured the diamond districts of Kono and elsewhere in Sierra Leone in 1992, he gave them the conduit for the diamond exports that would fuel their war and his own personal ambitions. Partnership Africa Canada's January 2000 report, *The Heart of the Matter: Sierra Leone, Diamonds and Human Security,* exposed the connection between diamonds and the continuation of war.

With enormous international attention focusing on Sierra Leone, and with the deployment of thousands of UN troops in the country by September 2000, Taylor shifted his attention to Guinea which, like Sierra Leone, shares long borders with Liberia, and which also possesses large diamond reserves. Exactly the same approach was applied to Guinea as had been applied to Liberia and then Sierra Leone. 'Rebels'—initially thought to be Guinean insurgents, but actually RUF and Liberian fighters— attacked across the border, feinting north at Forecariah and then moving more forcefully in the east, reaching within 100 kilometres of the country's diamond areas. As in Liberia and Sierra Leone, the economic objectives were two-fold: to deprive a legitimate government of the revenue it would need to fight back, and to gain access to resources that would add fuel to the conflict. *Destabilizing Guinea: Diamonds, Charles Taylor and the Potential for Wider Humanitarian Catastrophe*, a study of Guinea's crisis, produced by PAC in 2001, argued that 'Guinea's conflict, like the apparently waning one in Sierra Leone, is largely over resources— a rapacious and mercenary campaign for wealth.' The report said that Guinea's diamonds had become 'a magnet' for the predatory forces of Charles Taylor. At the time, the fighting—which had witnessed the destruction of some of its cities, the mass displacement of hundreds of thousands and the killing of thousands more—was treated by much of the international community as a humanitarian crisis, and not as part of the continuous narrative of escalating regional violence, with Taylor's Liberia as the primary instigator. Many even concluded that there might be a genuine rebellion against the undoubted corruption of Guinea's leadership. But no Guinean figure emerged to claim responsibility for the conflict, and when President Lansana Conté—a stubborn old soldier—mobilized his forces and resolutely beat the invaders back into Liberia and Sierra Leone, the 'rebellion' was heard of no more.

Taylor and Regional Destabilization

This was not the end of West Africa's linked crises, however. Liberia itself now erupted into violence after President Conté decided to arm and support anti-government Liberian dissidents based in his country. By the end of 2002, the rebel Liberians United for Reconciliation and Democracy (LURD) appeared to be largely contained, although fighting continued to flare episodically. But then Côte d'Ivoire, once a regional economic powerhouse, began to unravel, with the emergence of three 'rebel' factions following a failed coup attempt in September, 2002. There were reports of massacres and disappearances, and accusations by its beleaguered government, elected only two years before in a popular vote, that neighbouring Liberia and Burkina Faso were supporting anti-government militias. Côte d'Ivoire is the world's largest producer of cocoa, and it also has large reserves of timber. Most of these are concentrated in the west of the country, close to the Liberian border, and now the scene of fighting between Liberian-backed rebels and Ivorian government troops. Liberia's General Coocoo Dennis, a close aide of Taylor, and the man responsible for Taylor's logging operations in Grand Gedeh county—which is close to western Côte d'Ivoire—is believed to be the mastermind of 'rebel' activities in that part of Côte d'Ivoire. Both French and Ivorian intelligence reported in December, 2002, that former RUF commander and Taylor acolyte, Sam 'Maskita' Bockarie, was active there as well. That same month, long-simmering stories about an al Qaeda [a radical Islamist terrorist group] connection resurfaced. The *Washington Post,* citing a year-long investigation by various European intelligence agencies, reported that millions of dollars worth of West African diamonds had been bought by al Qaeda through channels arranged by Taylor and Burkina Faso's President Blaise Compaore, and that Taylor was paid $1 million for facilitating the deals. The study concluded that the bulk of the diamonds came from the RUF in Sierra Leone. The issue of the RUF and Taylor links to al Qaeda has been discussed in an earlier PAC study, and arises here only tangentially—in the context of the highly unregulated and corrupt nature of the wartime diamond industry in Sierra Leone, and the toxic nature and on-going criminality of Taylor and Compaore.

Recent [as of 2003] UN Expert Panel reports on Liberia have focused too narrowly on Taylor's role in Sierra Leone's war and the illegal diamond and arms trade. A more comprehensive approach focusing on Taylor's threat to wider regional stability is urgently required. In a detailed March 2003 report, Global Witness documents the Liberian government's role in setting up, arming and leading supposed Ivorian 'rebel' groups—the Movement for Justice and Peace (MJP) and the Ivorian Popular Movement of the Great West (MPIGO), both operating close to the Liberian border. According to Global Witness, the 'Liberian government has entrusted its closest and most experienced operatives for the insurgency in Côte d'Ivoire. These are individuals, such as Sam Bockarie, and logging companies, such as Maryland Wood Processing Industries (MWPI). They have been involved in planning, implementing and overseeing the operations.' The report also documents Liberian plans for a new 'two-pronged attack' on Sierra Leone which would involve 'activating cells of well-armed, Liberian paid operatives already within Sierra Leone, to be joined by an external force of Anti-Terrorist Unit (ATU) fighters attacking from Liberia.' The ATU, Taylor's elite security force, is now dominated by former RUF members. In the meantime, while Liberia goes without electricity and running water, Taylor is reported to have accumulated 'at a minimum, approximately US$3.8 billion from the illegal diamond and timber trades.' This money is said to be in Swiss bank accounts. A more recent report has demonstrated in great detail how West African diamonds have been used by Hezbollah [a Lebanese militant Islamist group] and al Qaeda to launder money and finance international terrorism.

A Peace Agreement Ends the Conflict in Liberia

Government of the Republic of Liberia, Liberians United for Reconciliation and Democracy (LURD), and Movement for Democracy in Liberia (MODEL)

The following viewpoint is part of the text of the peace treaty agreed to by the government of Liberia and rebel groups that ended the Liberian Civil War. The viewpoint declares a ceasefire, including disengagement and disarmament, to be monitored by international and regional bodies. The viewpoint explains that weapons are to be collected and secured, and that armed forces are to immediately disengage and cease hostilities.

Article II: Ceasefire

The armed conflict between the present Government of Liberia (GOL), the Liberians United for Reconciliation and Democracy (LURD) and the Movement for Democracy in Liberia (MODEL) is hereby ended with immediate effect. Accordingly, all the Parties to the Ceasefire Agreement shall ensure that the ceasefire established at 0001 hours on 18th June, 2003, results in the observation of a total and permanent cessation of hostilities forthwith.

Comprehensive Peace Agreement Between the Government of Liberia and the Liberians United for Reconciliation and Democracy (LURD) and the Movement for Democracy in Liberia (MODEL) and Political Parties, United States Institute of Peace, Peace Agreements Digital Collection, 2003. Reproduced with permission.

Article III: Ceasefire Monitoring

1. The Parties call on ECOWAS [Economic Community of West African States] to immediately establish a Multinational Force that will be deployed as an Interposition Force in Liberia, to secure the ceasefire, create a zone of separation between the belligerent forces and thus provide a safe corridor for the delivery of humanitarian assistance and free movement of persons.

2. The mandate of the ECOWAS Interposition Force shall also include the following:

   a. Facilitating and monitoring the disengagement of forces as provided under Article V of this Agreement;

   b. Obtaining data and information on activities relating to military forces of the parties to the Ceasefire Agreement and coordinating all military movements;

   c. Establishing conditions for the initial stages of Disarmament, Demobilisation and Reintegration (DDR) activities;

   d. Ensuring respect by the Parties for the definitive cessation of hostilities and all other aspects of the Ceasefire Agreement;

   e. Ensuring the security of senior political and military leaders;

   f. Also ensuring the security of all personnel and experts involved in the implementation of this Agreement in collaboration with all parties;

   g. Monitoring the storage of arms, munitions and equipment, including supervising the collection, storage and custody of battlefield or offensive armament in the hands of combatants;

3. The Joint Monitoring Committee (JMC) established under the terms of the Ceasefire Agreement, and composed

Jubilant cheers greet West African peacekeeping troops as they arrive in the town of Salala, Liberia, in September 2003. © AP Photo/Schalk van Zuydam.

of representatives of ECOWAS, the UN, AU [African Union], ICGL [International Contact Group of Liberia] and Parties to the Ceasefire Agreement shall continue to supervise and monitor the implementation of the Ceasefire Agreement.

4. Prior to the deployment of the International Stabilisation Force, a representative of ECOWAS shall chair the JMC [Joint Monitoring Committee].

5. The JMC shall:

   a. Resolve disputes concerning implementation of the Ceasefire Agreement, including the investigation of any alleged violation and also recommend remedial action for confirmed ceasefire violations.

b. Submit for approval, its recommendations to the Implementation Monitoring Committee (IMC) referred to under Article XXVIII(2) and (3) in this Agreement which is seized with the responsibility of monitoring the implementation of this Peace Agreement.

6. The Parties shall provide the JMC with any relevant information on the organisation, equipment and locations of their forces, and such information will be kept confidential.

Article IV: International Stabilization Force

1. The GOL, the LURD, the MODEL and the Political Parties agree on the need for the deployment of an International Stabilization Force (ISF) in Liberia. Accordingly, the Parties hereby request the United Nations in collaboration with ECOWAS, the AU and the ICGL to facilitate, constitute, and deploy a United Nations Chapter VII force in the Republic of Liberia to support the transitional government and to assist in the implementation of this Agreement.

2. The ECOWAS Interposition Force is expected to become a part of the International Stabilisation Force.

3. The Parties request the ISF to assume the following mandate:

a. Observe and monitor the ceasefire;

b. Investigate violations of the security aspects of this Agreement and take necessary measures to ensure compliance;

c. Monitor disengagement and cantonment of forces of the Parties and provide security at disarmament/cantonment sites;

d. Collect weapons at disarmament sites and elsewhere and ensure that the weapons so collected are properly accounted for and adequately secured;

e. Assist in the coordination and delivery of humanitarian assistance to displaced persons, refugees, returnees and other war-affected persons;

f. Facilitate the provision and maintenance of humanitarian assistance and protect displaced persons, refugees, returnees and other affected persons;

g. Verify all information, data and activities relating to the military forces of the Parties;

h. Along with ECOWAS and the International Contact Group on Liberia, provide advice and support to the Transitional Government provided for in this Agreement on the formation of a new and restructured Liberian Army;

i. Assist with security for elections;

j. Take the necessary means whenever the need arises and as it deems within its capabilities, to protect civilians, senior political and military leaders under imminent threat of physical violence;

k. Coordinate with ECOWAS in the implementation of this Agreement;

4. The Parties expect that units of the ISF shall be selected from countries acceptable to all the Parties to the Ceasefire Agreement.

5. The Parties to this Agreement call on the ISF to remain in place until otherwise determined by the UN Security Council and the elected Government of Liberia.

Children and the TRC

Building on the experiences of TRCs in other countries, particularly in Sierra Leone, the TRC Act referred specifically to children, noting their experiences during the conflict and their roles in the future development of the country. The Truth and Reconciliation Commission Act of 2000 that established the Sierra Leone TRC called for specific attention to be paid to sexual abuses and to the experiences of children, and for special procedures to address the needs of particular victims, but the Liberian TRC Act went into far greater detail. It set the stage for a concerted effort both to focus on the impacts of the conflict on children and to involve children in TRC activities.

The clear articulation of children's important role in the mandate, operation and outcomes of the TRC, and the call for policies, procedures and operational concerns to secure children's safe involvement in its work, were in themselves significant achievements. They raised new challenges and opportunities requiring human and financial resources, as well as a sustained commitment by the Commission to give primary consideration to the best interests of the child. Activities organized for children included awareness-raising workshops at county and district levels, statement-taking, and regional and institutional children's hearings.

Age was an issue that resisted satisfactory resolution. The Commission made a decision that all TRC children's processes would apply only to those who were eighteen or under at the time of the TRC activity, rather than at the time of their involvement in the war. This meant that many of those who had suffered as children during the conflict but who were over eighteen at the time of the TRC did not take part in the children's processes.

Theo Soua, "Children and the Liberian Truth and Reconciliation Commission," in Sharanjeet Parmar, Mindy Jane Roseman, Saudamini Siegrist and Theo Soua, eds., Children and Transitional Justice: Truth-Telling, Accountability, and Reconciliation, *Cambridge, MA: Harvard University Press, 2010, pp. 197–198.*

Article V: Disengagement

1. There shall be immediate disengagement of forces of the Parties to the Ceasefire Agreement in line with the principles of that Agreement.

2. Disengagement of forces shall mean the immediate breaking of tactical contact between opposing military forces of the GOL, the LURD, and the MODEL, at places where they are in direct contact or within range of direct fire weapons.

3. Immediate disengagement at the initiative of all military units shall be limited to the effective range of direct fire weapons. Further disengagement to pull all weapons out of range shall be conducted under the guidance of the ISF. The Parties to the Ceasefire Agreement undertake to remain in their disengagement positions until the conclusion of cantonment plans by the International Stabilisation Force and the NCDDRR [National Commission for Disarmament, Demobilization, Rehabilitation and Reintegration] established under Article VI(8) of the Agreement. They are also responsible for armed groups operating within their territories.

4. Where immediate disengagement is not possible, a framework and sequence of disengagement shall be agreed upon by all parties to the Ceasefire through the Joint Monitoring Committee (JMC).

5. Wherever disengagement by movement is impossible or impractical, alternative solutions requiring that weapons are rendered safe shall be designed by the ISF.

The Truth and Reconciliation Commission States Its Findings

Liberian Truth and Reconciliation Commission (TRC)

The Truth and Reconciliation Commission (TRC) is an organization created by the Liberian parliament and established in 2005 to investigate and report on the human rights violations that occurred during Liberia's twenty years of civil war and conflict. In the following viewpoint, the TRC states that all sides in the Liberian Civil War committed atrocities. It recommends against amnesty except for children who committed atrocities. It concludes that Liberia's future is in the hands of Liberians and that the TRC is the best way forward for Liberia.

This Report represents the Truth and Reconciliation Commission of Liberia's (TRC) forthright response to its core mandate of investigating and determining responsibility for 'egregious' domestic crimes, 'gross' violations of human rights and 'serious' humanitarian law violations as well as examining the root causes of Liberia's various episodes of state breakdown and violent conflicts to recommend measures to ensure that truth, justice and reconciliation become permanent features of Liberia's socio-economic, political, legal and cultural landscape.

Truth and Reconciliation Commission Final Report, December 3, 2009. Reproduced with permission.

A Troubled History

It aims to part a mountainous and depraved sea built on 186 years (1822–2006) of misunderstanding, inequality, poverty, oppression and deadly conflict with the enduring principles of truth, justice and reconciliation.

This Report provides the Liberian people, Government of Liberia and the Honorable National Legislature with substantive findings and determinations made by the TRC to date, knowing that two other volumes, Consolidated Report (Volume II) and Appendixes (Volume III) will be released by the TRC prior to the end of its mandate on June 22, 2009. The central rationale for issuing this Report prior to June is to provide the Liberian people notice of its findings and determinations to date in the wake of victims, thematic, actors and institutional-related hearings; notwithstanding that the actors and institutional hearings will continue through March 2009, as will its findings and recommendations.

Liberia's triumphant and tortuous history of conflict did not begin in January 1979 or end on October 14, 2003 (the TRC's temporal mandate period). Rather, the historical antecedents are woven deeply into its troubled socio-political and psychological culture. Until the November 8, 2005, run-off elections and subsequent inauguration of President Ellen Johnson-Sirleaf as Liberia's first post conflict democratically-elected president and Africa's first female democratically-elected president, Liberians were forced to live under various forms of oligarchic, autocratic, militaristic and authoritarian governments. In spite of the challenges of a verdant republic, the unsavory character of its various regime types, as Africa's first Republic and one of only two independent nations in Africa (Ethiopia being the other) throughout the colonial era, Liberia also served, among other things, as a sanctuary for Africans seeking to escape colonial oppression, an activist African nation while holding the presidency of the UN General Assembly in 1969, and a bulwark advocate against Apartheid in South Africa.

The Future of Liberia

Our Country's troubled and dichotomous history inevitably culminated into nationwide protest, chaos and mass violence in the late 1970's, a violent coup, military dictatorship and brutal repression in the 1980's, state breakdown, widespread deadly conflict and warlord politics in the 1990's, and a resurgence of violent conflict and scandalous corruption in the beginning of the 21st Century. Consequently, and as a means to identify the root causes of conflict in Liberia, protect fundamental human rights, end impunity and foster national healing, rehabilitation and reconciliation, the National Transitional Legislative Assembly of the National Transitional Government of Liberia—political bodies born out of the 2003 Comprehensive Peace Agreement (CPA)—acting under Article XIII of the CPA enacted the Truth and Reconciliation Act on June 10, 2005. The TRC began officially operating on February 22, 2006.

The Commissioners of the TRC feel very strongly that the future of Liberia rests with Liberians. While the international community has and will continue to play a role in assisting Liberia to develop a sustainable democracy, only Liberians can establish a durable human rights-based culture where peace, development and the rule of law are permanent features of its political heritage.

The Commission is convinced, as all Liberians are that the TRC framework provides the best opportunity yet, to review the past, learn from the past and lay the foundations for sustainable peace, justice and national reconciliation.

Jerome J Verdier, Sr
Chairman, TRC

The TRC Finds That:

1. The conflict in Liberia has its origin in the history and founding of the modern Liberian State.
2. The major root causes of the conflict are attributable to poverty, greed, corruption, limited access to education,

economic, social, civil and political inequalities; identity conflict, land tenure and distribution, etc.

3. All factions to the Liberian conflict committed, and are responsible for the commission of egregious domestic law violations, and violations of international criminal law, international human rights law and international humanitarian law, including war crimes violations.

4. All factions engaged in armed conflict, violated, degraded, abused and denigrated, committed sexual and gender based violence against women including rape, sexual slavery, forced marriages, and other dehumanizing forms of violations.

5. A form of both individual and community reparation is desirable to promote justice and genuine reconciliation.

6. Where in the determination of responsibility IHRL, IHL, ICL [International Human Rights Law, International Humanitarian Law, International Criminal Law], do not apply domestic criminal law statutes will apply.

7. No faction in particular instituted—in some cases to a very limited extent—adequate mechanisms to avoid or mitigate massive violations of human rights that characterized the conflict.

8. A form of both individual and community reparations is desirable to promote justice and genuine reconciliation.

9. All factions and other armed groups recruited and used children during periods of armed conflicts.

10. All factions engaged in armed conflict, violated, degraded, abused and denigrated, committed sexual and gender based violence against women including rape, sexual slavery, forced marriages, and other dehumanizing forms of violations.

11. Non derogation of rights during periods of emergency or armed conflict applies to the Liberian conflict situation.

12. Prosecution mechanism is desirable to fight impunity and promote justice and genuine reconciliation.

13. Common Article 3 and Protocol II of the Geneva Convention, having been ratified by the Government of Liberia apply to Liberia.

14. Liberia was engulfed in armed conflict from December 1989 to 1996; from 1999 to August 2003.

15. Preponderance of evidence is an appropriate evidentiary standard of proof appropriate to the work of the TRC considering that it is neither a criminal nor prosecuting institution.

16. Massacres, economic crimes, extra-judicial killings, for example, fall within the ambit of IHRL and IHL.

17. The New Penal Code of Liberia will apply as to mercenarism, official oppression, murder, kidnapping, rape, sexual assault, fraud in the internal revenue of Liberia, theft and/or illegal disbursement and expenditure of public money, counterfeiting, and misuse of public money, property or record.

18. Gross Human Rights Violations (GHRV) are generally, but not exclusively, committed by state actors, and may take place during times of peace or armed conflict, and can be directed against individuals or a group of individuals.

19. Lack of human rights culture and education, depravation and over a century of state suppression and insensitivity, and wealth accumulation by a privileged few created a debased conscience for massive rights violations during the conflict thus engendering a culture of violence as a means to an end, with an entrenched culture of impunity.

20. External State Actors in Africa, North America and Europe, participated, supported, aided, abetted, conspired and instigated violence, war and regime change against constituted authorities in Liberia and against the people of

Liberia for political, economic and foreign policy advantages or gains.

The TRC Determines That:

1. All warring factions are responsible for the commission of gross human rights violations in Liberia, including war crimes, crimes against humanity, IHRL, IHL, ICL, domestic criminal laws.

2. Prosecution in a court of competent jurisdiction and other forms of public sanctions are desirable and appropriate mechanisms to promote the ends of justice, peace and security, foster genuine national reconciliation and combat impunity.

3. The massive wave of gross violations and atrocities which characterized the conflict assumed a systematic pattern of abuse, wanton in their execution, and the product of deliberate planning, organized and orchestrated to achieve a military or political objective; disregarding the rights of noncombatants, children, and women, the elderly, disarmed or surrendered enemy combatants, etc.

4. All factions to the conflict systematically targeted women mainly as a result of their gender and committed sexual and gender based violations against them including, rape of all forms, sexual slavery, forced marriages, forced recruitment, etc.

5. Reparation is a desirable and appropriate mechanism to redress the gross violations of human rights and shall apply to communities and individuals, especially women and children, to help restore their human dignity, foster healing and closure as well as justice and genuine reconciliation.

6. General amnesty for children is desirable and appropriate. Amnesty for crimes lesser than gross violations is

also desirable and in certain circumstances appropriate to foster national healing and reconciliation.

7. IHRL, IHL, ICL, and Liberian domestic criminal statutes are applicable in establishing accountability for crimes committed during the mandatory period of the TRC work.

8. Reform of certain public institutions are appropriate to promote good governance and human rights, reduce poverty and alleviate illiteracy, promote peace, security, national reconciliation and opportunity for all.

9. While the TRC will not recommend general amnesty, except as provided in Count 5 above, the Commission however holds that all individuals admitting their wrongs and speaking truthfully before or to the TRC as an expression of remorse which seeks reconciliation with victims and the people of Liberia will not be recommended for prosecution.

10. Further investigations into matters under consideration by the TRC but remains incomplete up to the expiration of its tenure in June 2009 are desirable.

11. Liberians in the Diaspora are as much Liberians as Liberians at home; they continue to be engaged with developments on the homeland, supported, financed warring factions as an instrument for regime change; their voices must be heard and their issues and concerns must be addressed in fostering greater national reconciliation.

Charles Taylor Is Convicted of War Crimes

Associated Press

The Associated Press (AP) is an international, nonprofit news service. In the following viewpoint from a British newspaper, it reports that former Liberian president Charles Taylor's conviction for war crimes was upheld by an international war crimes court. Taylor was convicted of terrorism, murder, rape, and using child soldiers in connection with aiding and abetting rebel groups in Sierra Leone. The courts had found that Taylor received "blood diamonds" as payment for his assistance. The AP quotes a number of experts stating that Taylor's conviction sends a message that war criminals will be prosecuted and held to account.

An international war crimes court on Thursday [September 26, 2013] upheld the conviction and 50-year sentence of former Liberian President Charles Taylor for aiding rebels in neighbouring Sierra Leone, saying his financial, material and tactical support made possible horrendous crimes against civilians.

Associated Press, "Court Upholds Conviction for Former Liberian Leader Charles Taylor," *Globe and Mail*, September 26, 2013. Reproduced with permission.

Charles Taylor's Personal Background

Charles McArthur Taylor was born in Liberia in 1948, the son of an American father and Liberian mother. Through his mother's side of the family, Taylor is Americo-Liberian. The family lived until recently [as of 2003] in Clay-Ashland, a town just outside [of Monrovia] the capital [of Liberia]. Taylor attended Bentley College in Waltham, Massachusetts, graduating with a bachelor's degree in economics in 1977. He then moved to nearby Boston where he worked as a mechanic.

Despite his Americo-Liberian lineage, Taylor's political sympathies have long been with the indigenous people of Liberia. During his college years, he organized other exiled Liberians to oppose the Tolbert government, which was dominated by the politically powerful descendants of the first American settlers. He was thrilled when Samuel Doe took power in a coup, despite the vicious nature of his regime. Taylor returned to Liberia shortly after Tolbert's assassination in 1980 and joined Doe's administration. He headed the General Services Agency, whose principal function was the allocation of funds to government ministries, and was appointed a personal advisor to the president.

Taylor Held Accountable

The appeals chamber of the Special Court for Sierra Leone upheld the 65-year-old Mr. Taylor's conviction on 11 counts of war crimes and crimes against humanity including terrorism, murder, rape and using child soldiers.

Mr. Taylor's conviction in April 2012 was hailed as ushering in a new era of accountability for heads of state. He was the first former head of state convicted by an international war crimes court since World War II.

Mr. Taylor, wearing a black suit and gold-colored tie, showed little emotion as he stood while Presiding Judge George Gelaga King read the unanimous verdict of the six-judge panel. He is expected to serve his sentence in Britain.

Taylor remained in Liberia until 1983 when he fled to the United States amid allegations of corruption. The Liberian government charged that Taylor had embezzled US $900,000 from the government and they sought his extradition. A Boston court ruled that there was evidence to support the allegations, and Taylor was held in the Plymouth House of Corrections awaiting extradition to Liberia. In 1985, Taylor escaped from jail and fled to parts unknown, although there are some indications that he spent a large part of the next five years in Libya as the guest of Colonel Muammar al-Qadhafi.

From 1985–89, Taylor established his leadership of the NPFL [National Patriotic Front of Liberia] and prepared his Christmas Eve invasion, which subsequently launched a seven-year civil war. He established NPFL headquarters at Gbarnga, near the Liberian border with Guinea, and consolidated his control over the country. He created a new currency and banking system, developed an international airfield, and reestablished exports of diamonds, gold, rubber, and timber—in effect, he established a country within a country with himself as its warlord.

"Charles Taylor, President of Liberia." Worldmark Encyclopedia of the Nations. *11th ed., vol 6: World Leaders 2003. Detroit: Gale 2003.*

"Taylor's conviction sends a powerful message that those at the top can be held to account on the gravest crimes," said Elise Keppler of Human Rights Watch.

Steven Rapp, ambassador for war crimes issues at the U.S. Department of State—and former Prosecutor at the Sierra Leone court—said the ruling "sends a clear message to all the world, that when you commit crimes like this, it may not happen overnight, but there will be a day of reckoning."

The court found Mr. Taylor provided crucial aid to rebels in Sierra Leone during its 11-year civil war that left an estimated 50,000 people dead before its conclusion in 2002.

Thousands more were left mutilated in a conflict that became known for the extreme cruelty of rival rebel groups who gained

People scatter in fear as rebel troops fire mortar shells on the city of Monrovia, Liberia, on July 21, 2003. © Chris Hondros/Getty Images.

international notoriety for hacking off the limbs of their victims and carving their groups' initials into opponents. The rebels developed gruesome terms for the mutilations that became their chilling trademark: They would offer their victims the choice of "long sleeves" or "short sleeves"—having their hands hacked off or their arms sliced off above the elbow.

Blood Diamonds

Mr. Taylor was convicted not only of aiding and abetting Sierra Leone rebels from his seat of power in neighouring Liberia, but also for actually planning some of the attacks carried out by

Sierra Leone rebel groups the Revolutionary United Front and the Armed Forces Revolutionary Council. In return he was given "blood diamonds" mined by slave labourers in Sierra Leone and gained political influence in the volatile West African region.

Importantly, Thursday's ruling goes against an appeals decision by the International Tribunal for the Former Yugoslavia, in which former Serbian Gen. Momcilo Perisic was acquitted of aiding and abetting war crimes.

Judges at the ICTY said that in order to aid and abet a crime, a suspect has to have "specifically directed" aid toward committing crimes.

But judges in the Taylor case openly disagreed with that: they said the key to culpability for aiding and abetting a crime is that a suspect's participation encourages the commission of crimes and has a substantial effect on the crimes actually being committed—not the particular manner in which a suspect is involved.

CHAPTER 2

Controversies Surrounding Liberia

Chapter Exercises

PEOPLE WITH HIV/AIDS IN LIBERIA

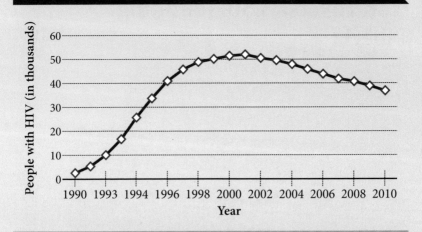

Source: Life Management Online, "Life Expectancy, HIV, AIDS Liberia."
www.lifemanagementonline.com.

Analyze the Graph

Question 1: How many people had HIV in Liberia in 1990? How many people had HIV in Liberia in 2000?

Question 2: What was occurring in Liberian politics between 1990 and 2000? In what ways might these events have affected a Liberian government response to the AIDS crisis?

Question 3: Did HIV rates rise or fall between 2003 and 2009? What political factors do you think contributed to this trend? What factors might have slowed this trend?

2. Writing Prompt

Imagine that you write for a blog that focuses on humanitarian issues. Write a post explaining why child soldiers should or should not face prosecution for the atrocities they commit in wartime.

3. Group Activity

Form two groups for a debate. One group should support and the other should refute the following statement: ECOWAS peacekeeping efforts reduced violence during the Liberian Civil War.

The Liberian War Was Fueled by Ethnic Tensions

Veronica Nmoma-Hilliard

Veronica Nmoma-Hilliard is an associate professor of African stud-ies at the University of North Carolina, Charlotte. In the following viewpoint, she traces the violence in Liberia to tensions between descendants of American black settlers (Americo-Liberians) and indigenous ethnic groups. She writes that Americo-Liberians con-trolled the government and oppressed other groups until the 1980 coup by Samuel K. Doe. Doe then proceeded to advance his own ethnic group, the Krahn, and attacked and brutalized other eth-nicities. She concludes that the civil war between Doe's regime and Charles Taylor's National Patriotic Front of Liberia quickly turned into a series of ethnic massacres.

A close analysis of the political conditions in pre-war Liberia provides insight into the refugee crisis. Liberia, about the size of Louisiana, was founded in 1822 by several US coloniza-tion societies supported by grants from the United States govern-ment. The two largest were the Maryland Colonization Society and the American Colonization Society. Driven by the abolition-

Veronica Nmoma-Hilliard, "The Civil War and the Refugee Crisis In Liberia," *The Journal of Conflict Studies,* University of New Brunswick, vol. 17, no. 1, Spring 1997. Reproduced with permission.

ist movement in the United States, Liberia was to serve as a place of refuge for freed American slaves. When Britain declared slavery illegal and enforced the ban by its powerful anti-slavery naval patrols, Liberia and Sierra Leone also became the places where "recaptured" Africans taken from vessels involved in the Atlantic slave trade were settled by the British.

A Mix of Peoples

Before the arrival of the settlers (Americo-Liberians), the territory now known as Liberia was an indigenous African socialist community. Civilization existed in the region prior to the arrival of the descendants of the settlers. The indigenous community had a government ruled by kings and village elders. Individuals were bound by institutional moral rules and laws, and stability was achieved through kinship and loyalty to the Poro society [an all-male secret society of both Sierra Leone and Liberia]. The community enjoyed high standards of social and political organization with institutions resembling those of the great medieval empires of Western and Central Sudan, in particular, Mali and Songhay.

Americo-Liberians comprised about 3 percent of Liberia's population during the early settler days. After the addition of "recaptured" Africans to the settlers, a new group emerged, akin to the Afrikaaners of South Africa, called "Congos" by the indigenous Liberians. This group also assimilated indigenous coastal people mainly from the Bassa, Kru and Grebo and evolved into an elite, educated minority group. Before 1870, the Americo-Liberians had been characterized by light-skinned persons who professed Christianity and controlled the reins of power. Thus, no dark-skinned person had been president of the country. E.J. Roye, the founder of the True Whig Party, was the first dark-skinned president to break the color-bar of the lighter-skinned Liberians.

The indigenous Africans consisted of several ethnic groups of which the largest are: Kpelle (298,500), Bassa (214,150), Gio (130,300), Mano (125,540), and Kru (121,400). Other smaller groups consist of: Grebo (108, 099), Gola (106,450), Loma (60,840), Bandi (30,870), Kissa (25,500), Vai (24,000), Krahn (18,464), Mandingo (over 10,836), Del (7,900), and Belle (5,386). The Bassa, Kru and Grebo are coastal "tribes" and were the first to encounter the early settlers. The Gola and Vai are close to the Sierra Leone border and, like the Mendi, are split between the two countries. The Mano and the Gio are interior "tribes" living on both sides of the border with the Côte d'Ivoire. The Krahn are split between Liberia and the Côte d'Ivoire. The Mandingo and Kpelle are found both in Guinea and Liberia.

Colonization and Inequity

The "tribal" Liberians were virtually colonized by the non-ethnic settlers or educated elite who considered them "primitive" or "heathens." The settlers took on the character of the slave masters and treated the indigenous population in like manner as they had experienced in slavery. They superimposed political, economic and social systems over the existing indigenous structures. With "tokenistic" education, the Africans were limited to nominal positions of no national social significance. Liberia's first president, Joseph Jenkins Roberts, kept most indigenous peoples from acquiring education in order to deter competition with the ruling elite class. He was in conflict with the protestant churchmen of Cape Palmas, "whom he accused of giving too much education to the Africans." Indigenous Liberians that occupied prominent positions in the government before 1980 were those affiliated to Americo-Liberians either through marriage, birth or servitude.

The ruling Americo-Liberian class practiced a system of patronage and dominated the country's politics for over a century (from 1870 until the military coup in 1980). It controlled the government and economy, owning over 60 percent of the country's wealth. Until recently [as of 1997], for example, senior legislative, judiciary and executive positions were retained

Fear of Ethnic Violence

In 1986, a Gio man told Bill Berkeley about his terror in Liberia of the Krahn, the late President Samuel Doe's ethnic community:

Just imagine. . . . They strip you. They put you down on the ground. They put a gun on your neck. And then they whip you. For nothing. Just because you are not Krahn. . . . Yes there will be revenge. These people are bad. The Krahn are too bad.

That same year a Krahn farmer told Berkeley that the Krahn too lived under fear of revenge:

We are in fact living in fear. We know that when power changes hands, everyone will suffer. What happens, the way Africans carry out politics, they will not make an exception for us. What I think is that, if there is an eventuality, if you know what I mean, there will have to be revenge. The situation in the country is very grave. We know that something will happen to us. We know that nothing lasts forever. We've got the feeling that something is in the making. When that thing explodes, then God have mercy on all of us.

Koigi Wa Wamwere, Negative Ethnicity: From Bias to Genocide, *New York, NY: Seven Stories Press, 2003, p. 136.*

by the elite families. In order to maintain a firm control on the system, relatives and family members of President William Tubman (1947–71) and President William Tolbert (1971–80) were appointed to important, crucial and sensitive positions. Tolbert's brother, Stephen Tolbert was Secretary of Agriculture and Commerce in Tubman's administration, and Minister of Finance under Tolbert's. During Tubman's administration, his son, Shad Tubman Jr., was President of the Confederation of Trade Unions. Equally, in Tolbert's government, his son was the Chairman of the House Foreign Affairs Committee, his son-in-law, Director of Budget, his cousin, Minister of Education, and his daughter, Assistant Minister of Education.

One-Party Rule

This small, privileged Americo-Liberian class also were members of one political party. Since 1870, the country was ruled by this sole party, the True Whig Party. For about a century, all attempts to establish an opposition party as stipulated in the Liberian constitution failed. Indeed, the Whig Party itself represented a "club" of individuals who were prepared to uphold and advance the privileges enjoyed by the minority Americo-Liberians in the country. [According to *The Liberian Crisis and ECOMOG*, edited by M.A. Vogt:] "All those who were not prepared to 'play the game' according to the rules of the Party were fenced out of the political, economic and social privileges that the elaborate patronage system could confer." Dr. Togba-Na Tipoteh, budget advisor to President Tolbert and also Professor of Economics in the University of Liberia identified with the plight of the masses and indigenous Liberians and lost both positions because of his refusal to be co-opted. President Tubman attempted to reverse some of the discriminatory policies toward the indigenous majority, but met with stiff resistance from the urban elite. In this regard, Gus Liebenow noted:

> The Americo-Liberian elite displayed an ambivalent political concern toward the involvement of tribal people in traditional forms of economic association. The involvement of tribal people in more modern forms of economic associations, on the other hand, was viewed with open hostility by the Whig leadership. In the absence of government support of cooperatives, the cash-crop economy was destined to remain under the control of foreign entrepreneurs and leaders of the Americo-Liberian class, with little competition from peasant cultivators.

This indigenous, oppressed class (the "tribal people") have long felt that their labor in iron ore, lumber and rubber plantations had benefited chiefly the elite class. In fact, there is no doubt that the oppressive rule by the elite minority for over 160 years was instrumental in setting the stage for the civil crisis. With an army of 5,000, of which more than 95 percent were "tribal," it seemed inevitable that the Liberian military coup would degenerate into a nightmare brought about by warring factions.

Samuel Doe's April 1980 Military Coup and Its Aftermath

The April 1980 coup, in which President Tolbert was assassinated, brought an end to the entrenched America-Liberian monopoly of power. As Okolo noted, Tolbert's attempt to suppress the opposition triggered the coup. The opposition formed two revolutionary movements: the Progressive Alliance of Liberia (PAL) and the Movement for Justice in Africa (MOJA). PAL, a radical organization, was formed in 1975 by Liberian students in the United States. It was determined to bring about a revolutionary change in Liberia by either violent or non-violent means. Like PAL, MOJA was a mass organization founded in 1973 in Liberia by students and professors of the University of Liberia. MOJA's objective was to raise the consciousness of workers, the urban unemployed, small cultivators, and students against Liberia's oppressive society.

PAL was legalized as an opposition party in January 1980, and renamed the Progressive People's Party (PPP). The PPP was determined to compete against the government's True Whig Party in both the legislative and presidential elections that were scheduled for June 1980 and 1983 respectively. Tolbert's government attempted to frustrate the chances of the PPP.

Although the PPP frustrated and threatened the survival of Tolbert's government, the real threat to Tolbert's administration occurred in April 1979, when his government announced a 50 percent increase in the price of rice, a national staple. This was followed by mass demonstrations against the price increase. The president called in his army and police, who opened fire on unarmed demonstrators, wounding about 400 people and killing between 40 and 140. In another major act of opposition to the government, the PPP in 1980 called for a nationwide strike until the Tolbert government resigned. Its leader, Gabriel Baccus

Krahn fighters fire at an area held by the National Patriotic Front of Liberia (NPFL) on the streets of Monrovia, Liberia, in May 1996. © Joel Robine/AFP/Getty Images.

Mathews, charged that Tolbert's government had failed to provide a better economic life for Liberians. In return, the administration arrested and detained leaders of the PPP charging them with treason. Months later, Sergeant Samuel Doe and his clique of non-commissioned officers of the Liberian army led a coup that overthrew Tolbert's government, thus, bringing an end to more than a century of True Whig Party dominance. Doe carried out bloody purges within the military establishment, and the execution of 13 cabinet members of Tolbert's administration was televised on the country's national television. Tolbert's body along with 27 members of his security force were dumped in a mass grave. Doe ordered all government officials who left before and after the April coup to return immediately and report to his government, or else face confiscation of properties in the country. However, in spite of Liberia's political problems, no large numbers of refugees were generated by the April coup.

Doe and Krahn Rule

Doe, on the other hand, was not very different from his predecessors. At first, his coup was welcomed by many Liberians. But his government's excessive violations of human rights, over-concentration of power, and rampant and uncontrolled corruption soon turned public opinion against him. His financial mismanagement left Liberia's treasury virtually empty, and nearly two billion dollars in debt. Doe came from the Krahn group which makes up about 4 percent of the Liberian population. He appointed some members of his ethnic group to senior government posts. Doe also recruited and promoted fellow Krahns within the armed force, which no doubt flared ethnic tensions within the army. As Mr. Diggs, former Liberian Ambassador to Nigeria noted:

> Every Krahn that was educated and aligned with Doe had a position in the government. In every office, Doe had a Krahn 'spy' who will approach you and say, 'Krahn by tribe; what is your tribe.' In fact, Krahn became almost the language of the governing circle in Liberia. If you did not speak Krahn, you are outside.

Along similar lines, Joyce contends that:

> Doe's great mistake, and the one that has had the most lasting impact, was his "ethnicizing" of the armed forces. Krahn people were given most of the authority in the military and the most significant posts in the government. The armed forces became almost completely Krahn and behaved more like a faction than a national army. Doe divided ethnic groups as never before.

There is no doubt that Doe's blatant discrimination and atrocities against other groups divided the country along ethnic lines. The Krahn dominated army was largely responsible for the atrocities and gross human rights violations committed during Doe's regime. Following a failed coup attempt by Thomas Quiwonkpa (a Gio whose ethnic group lived mainly in Nimba county), Doe's ethnic hatred led his army to engage in bloody reprisals, torturing and killing about 2,000 Gio and Mano civilians in Monrovia, Liberia's capital. Hundreds of soldiers from these two ethnic groups were also executed. Doe's revenge was not limited to the perpetrators of the coup but was extended to thousands of innocent civilians.

The civil conflict in Liberia, the first in the country's nearly 170-year history, began on Christmas Eve, 1989, when Charles Taylor and his National Patriotic Front of Liberia (NPFL) launched an invasion through northern Liberia from bases in Côte d'Ivoire (Ivory Coast). Taylor's objective was to overthrow the 10 year-old corrupt and dictatorial rule of Doe. His insurrection first started in Nimba, a county in north-eastern Liberia. In the first stage of the attack, Taylor and his NPFL limited their attacks to soldiers and government officials. However, Doe responded by mainly torturing, arresting and killing Gio and Mano civilians (the groups comprising most of Taylor's guerrilla support). Members of these groups began fleeing into neighboring Guinea in December 1989. About 13,000 sought refuge in Guinea, only a week into the civil war. Taylor's forces retaliated by attacking civilians of the Krahn and Mandingo ethnic groups. By the beginning of 1990, as the war intensified in Nimba and surrounding areas, some 120,000 refugees had fled to Côte d'Ivoire and Guinea.

Civil War and Ethnic Violence

Since 1989, the war has been largely a struggle for power among warring factions. What started as an attempt to oust Doe degenerated into ethnic massacres. The war fanned ethnic hatred as each faction fought with the desire to take revenge. Consequently, the course of the rebellion has changed into unrestrained killings on a mass scale and the number of displaced persons and refugees number over a million. Unfortunately, the war was not primarily a fight among combatants but a major onslaught on the innocent civilian population. It is ironic that the rebel factions that claimed to want an end to the anarchy in Liberia caused by Doe's army have themselves been inflicting needless suffering on the civilian populace they claimed to represent. This is not only peculiar to Liberia but has happened also in Sudan, Somalia, Mozambique and Angola.

Due to internal squabbles, one faction split from Taylor's NPFL in February 1990 to become the Independent National Patriotic Front of Liberia (INPFL). The INPFL headed by Prince Johnson competed with Taylor for the control of Liberia. As Taylor's rebel forces moved toward the capital, members of the Krahn and Mandingo ethnic groups as well as those who served in Doe's administration became victims of reprisals. The world stood by and simply condemned the indiscriminate massacres.

Contemporary War: Ethnic Conflict, Resource Conflict, or Something Else?

Isabelle Duyvesteyn

Isabelle Duyvesteyn is a professor at the University of Leiden and Utrecht University in the Netherlands. Her research focuses on military and security aspects of international affairs, terrorism, insurgency, humanitarian intervention, and the use of coercion as instrument of foreign policy. In the following viewpoint, she argues that ethnicity in Liberia is fluid and did not determine the civil war. Instead, she argues, the civil war was characterized by different political factions fighting for power. These factions sometimes tried to use ethnicity in order to mobilize armies, but the primary motivation was political. Charles Taylor, she concludes, was motivated by a desire for the presidency, and those who fought against him were working toward the political goal of keeping him out of office.

Contemporary war has been described as conflict between ethnic groups or concerned with control over resources and personal wealth. Although useful, the labels of ethnic war and resource conflict tend to bypass some important features of to-

Isabelle Duyvesteyn, "Contemporary War: Ethnic Conflict, Resource Conflict, or Something Else?," *Civil Wars*, vol. 3, no. 1, 2000, pp. 92–116. Taylor and Francis. Reproduced with permission.

day's conflicts. This article will argue that war as an instrument of politics, as originally formulated by Clausewitz, is still applicable to conflicts today. With the aid of empirical material from the conflicts in Liberia (1989–97) and Somalia (1988–95), it will be argued that, even when formal state structures have broken down, war can be a political instrument in the hands of warring factions.

War, for a long time, has been considered an instrument of politics.[1] It was seen as a continuation of politics with the admixture of other means.[2] War, it has been argued recently, is no longer exclusively an instrument of politics belonging to a state. War can be an instrument to gain, for example, wealth or to fight out ethnic rivalries used by groups and individuals. Contemporary war has been characterised by competition over resources or by ethnic strife.[3]

This article will argue that these ethnic and economic labels might be obscuring what is actually going on. Based on material from two African case studies, there is evidence that war can still be regarded as an instrument of politics, also when it is used by non-state actors.

The postulate that war is a continuation of politics by other means, was originally formulated by Major General Carl von Clausewitz. Clausewitz, writing in the nineteenth century about his experiences as a Prussian army officer during the Napoleonic Wars, saw war as made up of three elements: the government, the army, and the people. War is a political instrument at the disposal of government. The army can be used for the protection of the interests of government and people. The people provide the army with men and the support on which the government can rely to fight out the war. Clausewitz's ideas have guided warfare ever since. With the end of the Cold War, the ideas of Clausewitz have started to be questioned.[4] There are at least three apparently persuasive reasons for this.

First, contemporary war is marked in many cases by its civil or internal nature. As opposed to international wars which were

the focus of Clausewitz's ideas, civil wars are not fought out between states but within states.[5] Contrary to popular belief, these
wars are not a new phenomenon; civil war has been the dominant form of war at least since the end of the Second World War.[6]

Second, in these wars governments in power are not always
directly involved. Other groups than governments assemble
armies and participate in wars. These groups fight against each
other and the state may only contribute the delimitation of the
war by the maintenance of its borders.

Third, Clausewitz has not only been questioned because he
looked at a different kind of war and war concerned different en-
tities, but also because he identified war as a political instrument
which today has seemed less applicable. Wars can be fought, for
instance, for personal enrichment or for the safeguarding of ethnic interests. This article will assess the validity of this last point
of criticism in relation to Clausewitz. . . .

Ethnic Conflict

The end of the Cold War had many and far ranging effects. One
of them was the declining support for regimes in the developing
world which were previously thought to help contain commu-
nism. The ending of the foreign support had in some states the
effect of decreasing the state's ability to rule. In a few this resulted
in the collapse of the formal state structures, for example, Liberia
and Somalia. The wars that ensued were described as barbaric
with primeval forces being unleashed.[7]

The label ethnic war was popular to describe these conflicts.[8]
However, ethnicity is a problematic term. It has a very broad
definition, in which culture, religion, race, language, tradition,
tribe, heritage, history and myth are all used to define and de-
limit ethnicity. Some have noted that the term ethnic conflict is
now being used to describe all kinds of primitive looking conflicts in the world for which no other term is available.[9]

Furthermore, by using this term it is hoped that an explana-
tory value would be introduced. Ethnic conflict will here be

understood to be a conflict between groups consisting of individuals sharing a distinct identity on the basis of the above characteristics such as culture and history.

The way ethnicity was described by observers in the early 1990s, promoted the view that ethnic identity was an innate force which had been buried for the duration of the Cold War and re-emerged with force after its end. Whether ethnicity is an innate force or a social construct, is a topic for debate. Three broad schools of thought exist within the academic literature on ethnicity.

First, the primordialists argue that ethnic identity is a permanent element, members of a particular group are linked through a common bond which determines the identity of an individual.[10] This bond and identity create the coherence of the group. Ethnic identity can exist here without manifesting itself clearly but, it can be revived at any moment. The problem with this point of view is that the concept of ethnicity is seen as static.

Second, the instrumentalists see ethnic identity as a tool, and not as a permanent element.[11] Ethnic identity can be used and manipulated for political purposes. Constituencies can be created and people can be mobilised. The problem here is that individuals in practice are not completely free to choose their ethnic identity in the way they choose a political party. History and tradition must have some role here.

Third, constructivists present a middle ground.[12] They see ethnicity as changeable but only to a limited extent. Ethnicity is a construct of interactions in society, of existing social networks. Most primordialists, contrary to both the instrumentalist and constructivists, do see ethnicity as an inherently conflict promoting or producing element. Instrumentalists place emphasis on the role of leadership and elite, who use ethnicity to their own advantage. Constructivists see the role of social networks and social interaction outside of individual control as the link between ethnicity and conflict. Periods of transition, often marked by uncertainty, and ethnic problems have been found to be the most clear link between ethnicity and conflict.[13] The presence of two or more ethnic communities in a territory, however, does not automatically lead to conflict. Nor does a weak state mean that ethnic conflict is imminent.

There are several reasons to believe that attaching the label ethnic war to contemporary conflict has to be qualified. . . . First, caution is appropriate because in the anthropological literature, Liberian ethnic identity and Somali clan identity had a history of flexibility. Ethnic identity in Liberia seems to have had a history of fluidity before the outbreak of the conflict:

> it was not unusual for an individual to uproot himself from his own community and seek opportunities in another community headed by a chief of a different ethnic group, attaching himself to the household of a man of a different ethnic background and taking on that ethnic identity if necessary.[14]

Ethnic rivalry was used by President Doe when he took power in 1980 to justify the favours bestowed upon his ethnic group at the cost of the previously ruling group. Similarly, Taylor and his men argued that Doe had abused state funds long enough, now it was the turn of others. . . .

Although some claim the opposite, a primordialist argument is not tenable in either case, that is, ethnic and clan identity were not innate forces.[15] If an individual belonged to one clan or ethnic group in one situation and to another in a different set of circumstances, an innate identity is not present. The constructivists' argument is partly based on the same premise that ethnic and clan identity were a given but they were moulded in social networks. This has also been thought to apply in the two cases.

In Liberia, apart from the fact that an individual could change identity, social networks with a pre-formed identity on which the factions could rely for automatic support were not present. It is hard to find examples during the war of an organised network which the leaders could call on. There were no structures in

Liberian society which could be activated to support the invading forces. . . .

In Liberia, it has been argued that ethnicity started playing a more important role towards the end of the conflict.[16] In particular the split within ULIMO occurred along ethnic lines. However, in most instances the force of the ethnic factor seems to be less strong. Furthermore, it occurred frequently that fighters switched sides if other factions had more to offer.[17] If ethnic ties were the defining factor of the wars this could not occur. Membership of a faction was not exclusively based on ethnicity, and most factions included members of different ethnic groups. For the political negotiations the membership of a faction was more important than ethnic background.[18] Again, 'the ethnic labels generally attached to the various militias are ideological representations used by politicians as a means of creating constituencies'.[19]

A second reason to be cautious in applying the ethnic label to contemporary conflict is the following. The invading forces, in particular in Liberia, chose an area for their invasion which had a history of opposition to the government and had suffered under its retaliatory measures. However, calling on this local opposition potential on the basis of ethnic or clan identity had its limits. Taylor and his fellow dissidents consciously chose the area for their invasion which had been a hotbed of opposition against Doe. Only a few of Taylor's men belonged to the ethnic group dominant in the region. Taylor himself belonged to the elite of the pre-Doe days which had dominated Liberian politics since the foundation of the Liberian state.

During the invasion, ethnic identity was consciously put to use. This might signal that the NPFL men thought that, if they invaded in another area, they were not sure of getting enough support for their cause and would be more likely to fail. In effect, the support was slow in coming and the call on ethnic identity to support the invasion worked only to a limited extent.[20] What was more important in the creation of local support were

A soldier reacts after firing a rocket-propelled grenade at rebel forces near a bridge in Monrovia, Liberia, on July 23, 2003. © Chris Hondros/Getty Images.

the atrocities committed by the government army which tried to combat the invasion with retaliatory measures against the population.[21]

Summarising, the wars analysed here were ethnic or clan wars to the extent that they were made so by the factions. Ethnic and clan identity were highly flexible and fluid and the invaders consciously choosing an area where an appeal to ethnic identity might find fertile ground, were proven wrong. The invading forces called on identity to create a constituency in their fight to remove the regime in power. The fact that in both cases a mass uprising of the ethnic and clan groups failed to appear significantly undermines the primordialist and constructivist arguments. The appeal to a certain identity created the problem of narrow applicability, while the focus of the fighters was much wider, namely the state and the disagreements with the ruling elite. Therefore, the use of ethnic and clan identity sowed the seeds for the ultimate defeat of the invasions. Other groups were organised along the same lines, which made the goal of removing the regime and establishing a new presidency for the invading forces unattainable. . . .

War as a Continuation of Politics

As referred to in the introduction, Clausewitz's perspective of war as a political instrument available to states has lost attraction. Among the main reasons for the decline of this perspective were the observations that a formal state is not always present in contemporary war and that war might be an instrument for other purposes than political, as illustrated in the previous two sections.

This section will argue that war is still a political instrument, this time in the hands of factions.[22] Factions are potential states in the making. They are political units which use armed force to promote their aims and rely on people to fight in their ranks. Politics will be understood to be concerned with the organisation and procedures of groups (both intra- and inter-group relations) regarding the realm of the former state, that is, the organisation and control of the decision-making faculty which is aimed at the whole of a society. Even with the breakdown of the state, war can be seen as a continuation of politics with other means. Several reasons exist to assume that force remains a political instrument.

First, in both Liberia and Somalia, before the wars broke out, the channels for opposition were closed off. Opposition was not possible in Liberia under Doe. Exiles who were excluded from the rich pickings of the regime after falling out with Doe gathered in neighbouring countries. The invasion started a political process in which the population was called upon to make a political choice. The conflict did not fundamentally question the basis of power, which was authoritarian rule. It was more defined in negative terms of: no more Doe and his clique. Doe has had his time, now it was the turn of others. How the country should be ruled was less important than who should rule it. . . .

There were few other channels to influence, and wealth in both states which relied on highly personalised rule. The war was a continuation of politics but even more so it was a creator of politics. The invasion created opposition politics to the two regimes which was not possible before. All peaceful channels for changing the regimes had been exhausted and violence was an instrument in the hands of the politically motivated invaders to establish control over the state.

The political programmes of the factions were flimsy to say the least. They got their appeal from the opposition to the regime in power, which had lost credit by among others relying on a small group of the population. Taylor managed to get support for his plan to overthrow Doe, despite the fact that 'Taylor's force espoused no ideology beyond 'democracy' and opposition to Doe', he managed to draw 'significant support from Liberians united in their opposition to the Krahn (and Mandingo) rule of Samuel Doe'.[23] This support grew, as noted before, after the weakness the Doe regime showed in fighting the rebels. That Taylor was more interested in securing his own power than bringing democracy to Liberia, was clear even before the invasion[24]; 'The moment Charles Taylor entered Nimba the battle was for the mansion'.[25] However, this was overlooked, since all who participated in the invasion stood to gain by its success. When the regime was brought down, they would have a chance for wealth and influence by controlling the state.

Second, the predominance of political factors can be observed in the fact that the factions upon entering the country moved to the capital. Throughout the conflict the capitals were the centres of gravity. Taylor and his men encircled the capital and. . . . Taylor's alternative capital at Gbarnga did not manage to take away the focus on Monrovia. The old capital remained the legitimate seat of power and whomever controlled that would be seen to be in charge of Liberia, During 1992, the *de facto* presidency of Taylor was in danger from incursions from ULIMO, and the way out would be the capture of the presidential mansion. . . .

Third, political disagreements were one of the most important factors which kept the wars going. Political issues in particular who should rule and to a lesser extent how, were important bones of contention among the protagonists in the conflicts. Taylor had the ambition to become president of Liberia. When it became clear that Taylor was going to become the most likely contender, the INPFL and the ECOWAS states objected. The individual political disagreements and the striving for hegemony led to the continuation of the conflict after Doe's death.

Disagreements over who should rule the country created not only divisions among the parties but also within the parties. These divisions led to the creation of new factions. The INPFL was founded as a reaction, among others to Taylor's presidential ambition. New participants in the war, ECOMOG and ULIMO, both entered the battlefield to see their political wishes realised, namely to prevent Taylor from getting to where he wanted to be. . . .

Summarising, the conflicts were political to the extent that political issues provided the most important driving forces of the conflict. The invasion created a political process, which had not been possible before.

The factions moved for the capital which was seen as the seat of power and whomever could control this, would be in control of the country. The right to rule lay in the occupation of the presidential mansion. The disagreements over who should rule more than how the country should be ruled provided an important impetus in keeping the war going after the presidents were removed from power. War was initially a creator of politics and later on once a political arena had been created, war was a continuation of the fight over the exclusive control of politics.

Notes

1. This article is a summary of part of the author's PhD research at the Department of War Studies, King's College London. The distinction between war and conflict is often unclear. Some separate war from conflict by applying a threshold of 1,000 battle deaths before a conflict can be called a war. See, for example, *SIPRI Yearbook 1999* (London: Taylor & Francis 1999). This distinction will not be made in here and

conflict and war will be used interchangeably to describe the same phenomenon. Both are defined as armed interactions between at least two groups of which one can be, but not necessarily is a state or government in power. See also Isabelle G.B.M. Duyvesteyn, 'Een typologie van gewapende conflicten sedert 1945' (A Typology of Armed Conflict since 1945), *Transaktie* 26/2 (1997) pp. 186–94.

2. Carl Clausewitz, *On War* (London: David Campbell 1993). Also Martin van Creveld, *The Transformation of War* (NY: Free Press 1991).
3. See for examples of labelling wars as resource conflicts: David Keen, *The Economic Functions of Violence in Civil Wars*, Adelphi Paper 320 (London: IISS 1998). Ethnic wars: David A. Lake and Donald Rothchild (eds.) *The International Spread of Ethnic Conflict* (Princeton UP 1998). See also for wars of identity: Samuel P. Huntington, *The Clash of Civilizations and the Remaking of World Order* (NY: Simon & Schuster 1996).
4. van Creveld, *Transformation of War* (note 2).
5. In the academic literature civil wars have been relatively neglected. See Peter Wallensteen and Margareta Sollenberg, 'The End of International War? Armed Conflict 1989-1995', *Journal of Peace Research* 33/3 (Aug. 1996) pp. 353-70, p. 356.
6. The majority of quantified research seems to come to this conclusion: Frank Wayman, J. David Singer and Meredith Sarkees, 'Inter-state, Intra-state, and Extra-systemic Wars, 1816-1995', Paper presented at the 37th Annual Convention of the International Studies Association, San Diego California, 16-20 April 1996, p. 2. Wallensteen and Solenberg, 'The End of International War? (note 5). Klaus Jürgen Gantzel and Torsten Schwinghammer, *Die Kriege nach dem Zweiten Weltkrieg: 1945 bis 1992, Daten und Tendenzen* (Münster: Lit 1995) p. 117.
7. See for example Robert D. Kaplan, 'The Coming Anarchy; How Scarcity, Crime, Overpopulation, and Disease are Rapidly destroying the Social Fabric of Our Planet', *Atlantic Monthly*, Feb. 1994, pp. 44-76. And Daniel Patrick Moynihan, *Pandaemonium: Ethnicity in International Politics* (Oxford: OUP 1993).
8. Another related term to describe the new conflicts was religious war. However, the arguments on religious war focus mostly on a global struggle between Islam and other religions leading to international conflict as opposed to internal conflict. See Huntington, *Clash of Civilizations* (note 3). And John Esposito, *The Islamic Threat: Myth or Reality* (NY: OUP 1992). Also of interest is Mark Juergensmeyer, *The New Cold War? Religious Nationalism Confronts the Secular State* (Berkeley, CA: U. of California Press 1993).
9. Sam Rozemond, *Etnocentrisme* [Ethnocentrism] (The Hague: The Netherlands Inst. For Int. Relations 1994) p. 5.
10. Clifford Geertz, The Interpretation of Cultures: Selected Essays (NY: Basic Books 1973). John F. Stack Jr, 'Ethnic Mobilization in World Poltiics: The Primordial Perspective', in idem (ed.) The Primordial Challenge: Ethnicity in the Contemporary World (NY: Greenwood 1986).
11. Donald L. Horowitz, *Ethnic Groups in Conflict* (Berkeley, CA: U. of California Press 1985) p. 291.
12. Lake and Rothchild, *International Spread of Ethnic Conflict* (note 3).
13. Horowitz, *Ethnic Groups in Conflict* (note 19) p. 190.
14. Amos Sawyer, *The Emergence of Autocracy in Liberia: Tragedy and Challenge* (San Francisco, CA: Inst. For Contemp. Studies 1992) p. 54.
15. For the primordialist argument on the Liberian war see Conteh-Morgan and Kadiver, 'Ethnopolitical Violence in the Liberian Civil War' (note 12) p. 41. For Somalia see

Ioan M. Lewis, *Blood and Bone: The Call of Kinship in Somali Society* (Lawrenceville, NJ: Red Sea 1994).

16. See for example Kenneth Noble, 'Liberia's Fragile Peace Shows Signs of Fraying', *International Herald Tribune*, 6 Nov. 1993; James Butty, 'Reign of Terror', *West Africa*, 4 July 1994 and Phillip van Niekerk, 'Hundreds Die as Warlords Clash in Power Struggle', *The Observer*, 7 April 1996.
17. Human Rights Watch, *Easy Prey: Child Soldiers in Liberia* (NY: Human Rights Watch 1994) p. 29-30. William Reno, 'Reinvention of an African Patrimonial State: Charles Taylor's Liberia', *Third World Quarterly* 16/1 (1995) pp. 109–20, pp. 116–17.
18. Anthony Clayton, *Factions, Foreigners and Fantasies* (Camberley: Conflict Studies Res. Centre 1995) p. 17.
19. Ellis, 'Liberia 1989–1994' (note 9) p. 183.
20. Gerald Bourke, 'Liberian Battles, "Spreading South"', *Independent*, 19 Jan. 1990. And Mark Huband, 'US Advisors Help Liberia Deal with Rebels', *Financial Times*, 30 Jan. 1990.
21. Johnathan C. Randal, 'For Liberia Leader, a Revolt that Won't Go Away', *International Herald Tribune*, 20 March 1990.
22. Douglas Rimmer argues that wars in Africa during the Cold War have been also mostly political undertakings. See Douglas Rimmer, 'The Effects of Conflict II: Economic Effects', in Furley, *Conflict in Africa* (note 56) pp. 295-313, p. 303. For more on Clausewitz and van Creveld and the role of politics of the state see Jan Geert Siccama, 'Clasuewitz, Van Creveld and the Lack of a Balanced Theory of War', in Gert de Nooy (ed.) *The Clausewitzean Dictum and the Future of Western Military Strategy* (The Hague: Kluwer Law Int. 1997) pp. 25-42.
23. Herbert Howe, 'Lessons of Liberia ECOMOG and Regional Peacekeeping', *International Security* 21/3 (1996) pp. 145–76, p. 149.
24. Cameron Duodu, 'Liberia Hostage to Tribalism as Final Battle Looms', *The Observer*, 3 June 1990.
25. Doe's deputy information minister, Paul Allen Wie quoted in Huband, *Liberian Civil War* (note 11) p. 167.

The Sierra Leone/Liberian Conflict Was Fueled by the Diamond Trade

James Rupert

James Rupert is a correspondent for the Washington Post. *In the following viewpoint, he reports on connections between the diamond trade, Sierra Leone, and Liberia. He argues that control of diamond resources has been a major cause of conflict in the two countries. He also suggests that Liberia president Charles Taylor aided the Sierra Leone rebels in return for diamonds, which are often smuggled out of Sierra Leone through Liberia to be shipped to buyers overseas. Rupert also implicates neighboring Burkina Faso in the corruption and violence around diamonds in the region.*

When Sierra Leone's lone combat helicopter blew an engine one day last year [1998], it meant disaster for the government. The aging Soviet-built gunship had been the government's most effective weapon against a rebel army that was marching on the capital, burning villages and killing and mutilating civilians.

James Rupert, "Diamond Hunters Fuel Africa's Brutal Wars," *Washington Post,* October 16, 1999. From *The Washington Post*, October 16, 1999, copyright © 1999 by the Washington Post Company. All rights reserved. Used by permission and protected by the Copyright Laws of the United States. The printing, copying, redistribution, or retransmission of this content without express written permission is prohibited.

Hunger for Diamonds

Officials scrambled to repair or replace the helicopter. But rather than relying on conventional arms dealers, they took bids from mining companies, gem brokers and mercenaries, most of whom held or wanted access to Sierra Leone's diamond fields. The government finally agreed to buy $3.8 million worth of engines, parts and ammunition through a firm set up by Zeev Morgenstern, an executive with Belgium-based Rex Diamond Mining Corp.

In the end, the parts proved unsuitable, and the helicopter stayed grounded. The rebels of the Revolutionary United Front (RUF) seized Freetown, killing thousands of residents and—in their signature atrocity—amputating the arms or hands of hundreds of civilians.

Although the government later retook the capital, the rebels' success forced the government this summer [1999] to accept a deal to share power. Though controversial, the peace agreement has drawn enough U.S. and other international support that Secretary of State Madeleine K. Albright will visit here Monday on the first day of an African tour.

The key role of mining interests in the fighting was nothing new in Sierra Leone. The eight-year conflict that has shattered this country and brutalized its 5 million people has been fueled by foreigners' hunger for diamonds. Rival mining companies, security firms and mercenaries—from Africa, Europe, Israel and the former Soviet Union—have poured weapons, trainers and fighters into Sierra Leone, backing the government or the rebels in a bid to win cheap access to diamond fields.

Across Africa, foreign firms are fueling wars for natural resources that in some ways recall the 19th-century "scramble for Africa" by European imperial powers. Since the end of the Cold War—when major countries pulled back from African conflicts—oil and mining companies, security firms and mercenaries have filled the void. They have provided arms and expertise for civil wars in Angola, Congo, Liberia and here.

Diamonds Prolong War

These conflicts are singularly brutal, scholars say, because many of their sponsors are outsiders with little motive to limit destruction. The superpower patrons of Cold War conflicts "did not allow the wholesale ripping up of the economy, the use of children as soldiers, the attacks on relief groups" that have become the norm in Sierra Leone and elsewhere, said Herbert Howe, a Georgetown University political scientist.

In Sierra Leone, both the government and the RUF have attracted military backers by offering payment in diamonds or diamond-mining rights. The fortunes to be made from such ventures have prolonged and escalated the war, analysts say. According to documents and African, U.S. and European sources, the spoils have also encouraged the involvement in the conflict of a number of prominent foreigners:

> Charles Taylor, president of Sierra Leone's neighbor, Liberia, and his son, Charles Jr., have helped the RUF obtain foreign arms and military training, said African and Western military intelligence sources and Liberians. An American with military experience described watching at Liberia's main airport as members of one of the president's security forces supervised the unloading of two truckloads of automatic rifles and ammunition that he said were then sent to the Sierra Leonean border.

A Liberian government spokesman denied that Taylor or his son had provided weapons to the RUF, or had interests in Sierra Leone's diamond trade. International diamond merchants and other sources say that by helping the RUF control Sierra Leone's diamond fields, Liberia can divert more Sierra Leonean diamonds through its territory on the way to world markets, reaping part of the profits.

A retired South African army intelligence officer, Fred Rindle, has provided training to Taylor's forces and to the RUF, African and Western military sources say. Rindle, who also

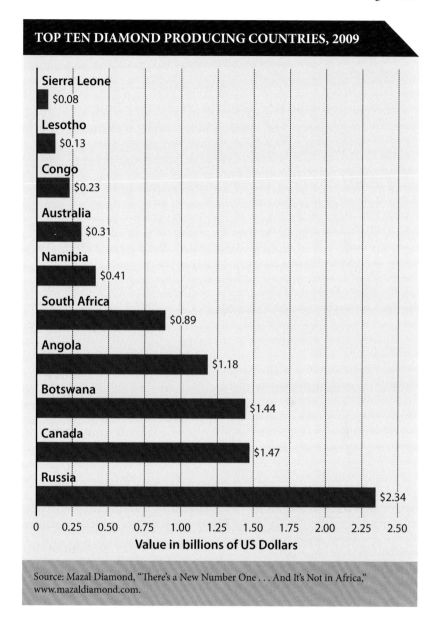

TOP TEN DIAMOND PRODUCING COUNTRIES, 2009

Sierra Leone $0.08

Lesotho $0.13

Congo $0.23

Australia $0.31

Namibia $0.41

South Africa $0.89

Angola $1.18

Botswana $1.44

Canada $1.47

Russia $2.34

Value in billions of US Dollars

Source: Mazal Diamond, "There's a New Number One . . . And It's Not in Africa," www.mazaldiamond.com.

helped arm UNITA rebels in Angola, is also exporting diamonds from Liberia, according to other African and Western sources.

A Ukrainian businessman, Leonid Minin, has supplied arms to Taylor and the RUF, according to a senior officer of the West

African peacekeeping force in Sierra Leone. Minin, who is well connected to government officials in Ukraine, operates a timber company in Liberia that also is dealing in arms and diamonds, according to the officer and Liberian sources.

Morgenstern, the Rex Mining executive, and the company's Antwerp-based president, Serge Muller, set up a company to sell weapons to the Sierra Leonean government, which has granted Rex several diamond mining leases. In separate interviews, Morgenstern and Muller said the arms deals were unrelated to Rex's mining activities.

A retired Israeli army officer, Yair Klein, has provided military material and training in Liberia and Sierra Leone since 1996, according to West African sources and the Israeli newspaper Yedioth Aharonoth. Israel convicted Klein in 1991 of illegally selling arms and training to Colombian groups that the Colombian government says were fronts for the Medellin cocaine cartel.

Klein competed with Morgenstern last year for a helicopter contract in Sierra Leone while seeking mining rights, according to Yedioth Aharonoth. Sierra Leone arrested Klein last January and is trying him for alleged fraud in the proposed purchase of a helicopter from Belarus.

Mired in Corruption

Sierra Leone's war began in 1991 when a dismissed army corporal, Foday Sankoh, formed the RUF and led a rebellion against the authoritarian rule that had mired this country in poverty and corruption. The RUF briefly attracted students to its cause, but soon alienated most Sierra Leoneans with brutal tactics.

The role of outsiders in the fighting began in earnest in 1995, when Sierra Leone's then-military government hired a South African firm, Executive Outcomes. The company effectively was a military battalion for hire—one of the most prominent of a new generation of private military corporations. It brought in a few hundred fighters, most of whom were veterans of the South African army, who drove the RUF out of the major diamond fields and destroyed some of their key jungle strongholds.

While Sierra Leone paid Executive Outcomes to fight the rebels, the government also awarded diamond-mining rights to Branch Energy, a firm linked to Executive Outcomes through cross-ownership among a group of former South African and British military officers. While Executive Outcomes provided security in Kono, the country's richest diamond region, Branch Energy mined there.

Executive Outcomes' victory allowed Sierra Leone to hold elections in March 1996 for a civilian government whose president, Ahmad Tejan Kabbah, signed a peace accord with the weakened RUF in late 1996. Under the deal, Kabbah ended Executive Outcomes' contract in 1997.

Less than four months later, Sierra Leonean soldiers angry about their poor pay ousted Kabbah in a coup and invited the RUF to join them in power. The army and the RUF conducted a nine-month reign of terror in which soldiers and guerrillas roamed Freetown at night, robbing and raping residents in what they called "Operation Pay Yourself."

Last year, Kabbah turned again to outsiders—chiefly an old ally, Nigeria. Under the flag of a West African peacekeeping force, ECOMOG [Economic Community of West African States Monitoring Group], Nigeria sent thousands of troops to a February 1998 offensive to oust the junta [military-led government] and return Kabbah to power.

Kabbah hired a British military company, Sandline International, to back the Nigerians, according to a report in July by a British government investigator. A Thai businessman, Rakesh Saxena, agreed to pay $10 million to finance Sandline's role, in exchange for mining rights in Sierra Leone. But Saxena was on the run in Canada from a Thai arrest warrant, and he delivered only $1.5 million for Sandline before he was arrested in Canada, said the investigator, Sir Thomas Legg.

With logistical help from Sandline, Nigerian troops and pro-Kabbah militias forced the RUF out of Freetown in February, 1998, but failed to win back all of the Kono diamond region. For months, both armies dug diamonds furiously, said Nigerian and Sierra Leonean sources.

Despite a government order suspending all mining, Nigerian officers in Kono quickly put local diamond diggers back to work under their control. Nigerian soldiers complained that officers were neglecting the troops, spending their time and ECOMOG money to run mining operations.

Reports of Rearming

While some Nigerian officers mined gems, Nigerian military intelligence monitored signs that the RUF was rearming. The Nigerians and a Western intelligence agency tracked aircraft that they said had been seen transferring crates of arms at West African airfields. Many flights came from Eastern Europe, most often making stops at Ouagadougou, the capital of Burkina Faso, said Maj. Gen. Felix Mujakperuo, ECOMOG's commander until this summer. From Ouagadougou, a few planes flew directly to airstrips in rebel-held zones of Sierra Leone, but most flew to Liberia's Robertsfield International Airport.

U.S. officials have said they have evidence that Liberia and Burkina Faso have been helping arm the rebels. The Washington Post obtained the registration numbers of five aircraft that ECOMOG said had carried weapons to the RUF. When the numbers were checked against an international registry of commercial aircraft compiled by Airclaims Ltd., a private firm, the registration of one of the planes matched that of a Boeing 727 owned by the government of Burkina Faso.

The RUF denies receiving any significant armament from abroad. It gets nearly all its weapons by capturing them from government forces, said RUF spokesman Omrie Golley.

In March 1999, Mujakperuo said, Ukrainian-operated aircraft shipped arms for the RUF via Ouagadougou airport's VIP terminal. Burkina Faso has denied accusations, including some from U.S. officials, that it has aided the RUF.

Two military intelligence agencies reported intercepting communications from RUF commanders to Liberian officials confirming the receipt of arms or other assistance. A senior officer of ECOMOG said a logging company run by Minin, the Ukrainian, has trucked arms to the RUF under the cover of its timber operations near the Sierra Leonean border. Minin's Monrovia firm—Exotic Tropical Timber Enterprise—exports logs, but "their real business is diamonds and arms supply," he said.

A company official did not return phone calls asking about its operations. Minin, who also operates a firm in Zug, Switzerland, did not return a call to his office there.

Smuggled Through Liberia

The U.S. government estimates that smuggled African diamonds represent 10 percent to 15 percent of the global diamond trade, a State Department official said, a share worth $5 billion to $7 billion per year at current prices. Sierra Leone probably produces $300 million to $450 million worth of diamonds each year, said Caspar Fithen, a specialist on Africa and diamonds at Oxford Analytica, a British research firm.

Sierra Leone exports "a very, very marginal part" of its diamonds through its official channels, said Lawrence Ndola Myers, acting director of Sierra Leone's Government Gold and Diamond Office. Myers and diamond industry analysts in Europe said most of Sierra Leone's diamonds are smuggled through Liberia, which is exporting vastly more stones than its mines could be producing, as well as through neighboring Guinea.

Liberian officials, including Mines Minister Jenkins Dunbar, did not deny that RUF-produced diamonds might be exported through Liberia, but said his government had no figures on Liberian diamond production or exports.

In Belgium, the world's largest market for rough diamonds, a total of 8.3 million carats of stones, worth $601 million, were imported from Liberia during 1997 and 1998, according to the Antwerp High Diamond Council. But the U.S. Geological Survey, which monitors global mining, estimates that—based on the known state of Liberia's diamond fields and mining industry—the country can produce only about 60,000 carats per year of rough gemstones, said Philip Mobbs, an Africa specialist at the agency. In Antwerp, diamond buyers routinely "are labeling Sierra Leonean stones as Liberian," said Chris Gordon, a diamond industry analyst in London.

African and Western military sources say Liberia's Taylor or his son have recruited business associates to help the RUF. In the late summer of 1998, Charles Taylor Jr., who helps run his father's security apparatus, asked foreign military trainers working for him to help with a "cross-border project," said a Western military specialist who asked not to be named. "Chuckie was indirect . . . [but] he made it clear that the project was to help the rebels in Sierra Leone," the source said.

President Taylor's press secretary, Reginald Goodridge, repeated government denials that Liberia has helped the rebels, saying "this issue has been put to rest. We've cooperated in bringing the [Sierra Leonean] sides together."

When the RUF's offensive began in late 1998, the rebels used "textbook South African army" tactics, said a South African military source. Several African and Western military sources said they believe this was the result of training by Rindle, the former intelligence officer.

Under apartheid, Rindle served as a South African army liaison officer to the Angolan rebel movement, UNITA. After South Africa ended its support of UNITA, Rindle continued to help them on his own, getting paid in diamonds, according to South African and U.S. intelligence sources.

Since at least 1998, Rindle has spent a lot of time in Liberia, with his transportation and hotel accommodations arranged by Charles Taylor Jr., according to sources in Monrovia. "On some trips, he has come with teams of South African soldiers and gone with them into the bush," said one source.

Diamond-Mining Deal

In July [1999], Rindle, a quiet, dapper man, spent several days at Monrovia's most exclusive hotel with a leading South African geologist, Morris J. Viljoen of the University of Witwatersrand, and two other South Africans. They were heard discussing plans for a diamond-mining deal with Charles Taylor Jr. When Rindle subsequently was asked one morning for an interview there, he said he was in the country on mining business. He agreed to a meeting that evening, but instead checked out of the hotel.

No Liberian official would discuss Rindle or his relationship with Charles Taylor Jr.

Late last fall [1998], the RUF launched what became its most brutal offensive of the war. It seized full control of Kono, surprising ill-prepared Nigerians. Defeated at Kono, ECOMOG collapsed and the rebels reached Freetown. In July [1999], the government signed a deal with the RUF that gives the rebels seats in the cabinet and amnesty for crimes committed during the war. It also places Sankoh, the rebel leader, in charge of a commission that will help decide who will get to mine Sierra Leone's minerals, including diamonds.

Child Soldiers Should Not Be Prosecuted for War Crimes

David M. Crane

David M. Crane is a professor at Syracuse University College of Law and the founding chief prosecutor of the Special Court for Sierra Leone. In the following viewpoint, he argues that the use of child soldiers is an international crime and should be prosecuted as such. He notes that the Special Court for Sierra Leone decided not to prosecute soldiers under age eighteen for atrocities. Crane argues that this was the correct decision and says that it should set an international precedent, encouraging the rehabilitation of child soldiers rather than their prosecution.

The use of children in warfare is not a new phenomenon. Children have followed armies for centuries as support personnel—as pages, water carriers, and musicians, particularly drummers. In navies throughout Europe, nobility seconded children to warships to learn a trade. Others were pressed into seamanship.

Children, War, and Law
With the advent of The Hague rules governing weapons in war in the late nineteenth and early twentieth centuries, the rules of

David M. Crane, "Prosecuting Children in Times of Conflict: The West African Experience," *Human Rights Brief*, vol. 15, no. 3, 2008, pp. 14–15. Reproduced with permission.

warfare took on a universal status. Coupled with the Red Cross movement, the role of the combatant became a legal term of art. The status of the non-combatant also began to take shape. Yet specifics regarding combatants' ages were not well-defined early in the regulation process. The international community focused more on regulating weapons that would cause unnecessary suffering and the types of targets combatants could engage.

After World War I and into World War II, the shift away from universal rules relating to weapons and targets began. By the end of the two wars, the focus was rightfully on non-combatants. The founding of the UN in 1945 created a permanent body that could be a voice for non-combatants, particularly for children.

The universal rules began to narrow and define the special status of non-combatants. The Geneva Conventions of 1949 are the cornerstone of these rules, which by their nature, protect persons who are "out of the combat"—prisoners of war, the shipwrecked, and civilians. It is here that children became specially protected under international law. Around this time the international community laid out international human rights principles in the Universal Declaration of Human Rights, which echoes fundamental principles of human dignity found in the Geneva Conventions. The world had a new standard for protecting non-combatants' rights and status in wartime.

One of the tragedies of the ensuing Cold War was the conflicts ignited in developing country "flashpoints." Children were once again the victims. In the 1970s, the world paused long enough to reconsider the Geneva Conventions of 1949, shaping them through two new protocols to reflect the realities of modern armed conflict. Once again the bar had been identified and raised. Most of the nations of the world, including many newly independent states, agreed to the new standards.

The Protocols specifically prohibit the use of children in armed conflict. The criminality of the act of using children in conflict, however, is not specifically laid out. The implication is that violating the Geneva Conventions' provisions related to civilians as non-combatants implies a grave breach when using children in combat. Such breaches impose a duty to investigate and prosecute upon all signatories.

The Convention on the Rights of the Child

The subsequent adoption of the Convention on the Rights of the Child (CRC) highlights the prohibition against the use of children in armed conflict. It is my judgment that the CRC criminalizes the concept of child recruitment. One can argue that child recruitment as a crime is reflective of customary international law. The CRC requires national jurisdictions to establish a minimum age at which criminal responsibility may be assigned. Article 1 of the CRC defines children as *"all human beings below the age of 18."* Additionally, the CRC Optional Protocol II admonishes armed groups that are distinct from armed forces of a state not to recruit or use in hostilities, under any circumstances, persons under 18. The applicable international agreements also cover the detention of delinquents and the issues related to this stage of the juvenile justice process.

Despite states' political and legal recognition that child recruitment was a universal crime and that children had a special status in conflict, child recruitment continued unabated. Millions of children died in the 1980s and 1990s, mainly in Africa where children played a significant role in armed conflicts. The 1996 Secretary-General's report on this issue stunned the UN by highlighting the extent of the problem throughout the world. There were calls for action and an evolving plan emerged to monitor recruitment of child soldiers.

In the late 1990s, the international community began to develop a mechanism to prosecute war crimes and crimes against humanity. The Rome Statute created the ICC [International Criminal Court], which is now the world's attempt to stamp out impunity. The Rome Statute specifically states that the recruit-

A child soldier of Liberians United for Reconciliation and Democracy (LURD) hands over his weapon to a UN peacekeeper in Gbarnga, Liberia, in April 2004. A special court decided not to prosecute soldiers younger than eighteen. © AP Photo/Pewee Flomoku.

ment of children under the age of 15 is a "serious violation of international humanitarian law."

The Decision Not to Prosecute the Child Soldiers of West Africa

The Statute of the Special Court gives the Prosecutor authority to indict children for crimes they committed between the ages of 15 and 18. The basis for including this controversial provision was to give the Prosecutor legal authority to prosecute any child soldier he might consider as having borne the greatest responsibility for war crimes and crimes against humanity committed during Sierra Leone's civil war.

The Prosecution decided early in developing a prosecutorial plan that no child between 15 and 18 had the sufficiently blameworthy state of mind to commit war crimes in a conflict setting. Aware of the clear legal standard highlighted in international humanitarian law, the intent in choosing not to prosecute was to rehabilitate and reintegrate this lost generation back into society. It would have been impractical to prosecute even particularly violent children because there were so many. Further, it was imperative that the prosecution seriously consider the clear intent of the UN Security Council and the drafters of the Statute creating the Court to prosecute those and *only* those who bore the greatest responsibility—those who aided and abetted; created and sustained the conflict; and planned, ordered, or directed the atrocities. No child did this in Sierra Leone.

In November 2002, the Prosecution announced that child soldiers would not be prosecuted, as they were not legally liable for acts committed during the conflict. There was universal praise for this decision. It took prosecuting child soldiers themselves for the tragedy they have experienced off the legal table, instead placing children on the rehabilitation track, as is the appropriate norm under international law.

Should Child Soldiers Be Prosecuted for Their Crimes?

IRIN

IRIN is a United Nations news service focusing on humanitarian stories in regions lacking such coverage. The following viewpoint discusses the confused status of child soldiers in international law. The exact age at which combatants are considered child soldiers is left up to individual states. The lack of consistency can be seen as weakening international standards. The viewpoint also argues there is general agreement that child soldiers should not be prosecuted but points out that this raises problems as, in some cases, child soldiers may be ordered to commit particularly heinous crimes because they are not likely to be prosecuted.

International human rights law meanders between the vague and the hazy when it comes to its stance on the age of criminal responsibility and what, if any, punishments should be imposed on child soldiers guilty of war crimes.

The godfather of human rights laws, the Geneva Conventions, oblige all member states to act on grave breaches of human rights, but does not stipulate the age of criminal responsibility.

IRIN, "Should Child Soldiers Be Prosecuted for Their Crimes?," October 6, 2011. Reproduced with permission.

Robert Young, deputy permanent observer and legal adviser to the International Committee of the Red Cross (ICRC) based in New York, told IRIN international humanitarian law (IHL) remains "silent" on the age of responsibility for perpetrators of grave human rights abuses, such as willful killing, torture and inhumane treatment.

International Criminal Court (ICC) Article 26 prevents the court from prosecuting anyone under the age of 18, but not because it believes children should be exempt from prosecution for international crimes, "but rather that the decision on whether to prosecute should be left to States," says the Office of the Special Representative of the Secretary-General (SRSG) for children and armed conflict (Working Paper Number 3: Children and Justice During and in the Aftermath of Armed Conflict, September 2011). "[The] exclusion of children from the ICC jurisdiction avoided an argument between States on the minimum age for international crimes," it noted.

The age of criminal responsibility varies from country to country, from 7–16, but the bar is most commonly set at 14.

Although IHL does not set a minimum age for criminal responsibility for international crimes, it is argued that a yardstick has been laid down for some form of indemnity through IHL's recognition that recruitment of child soldiers under 15 was a war crime.

The Children and Justice During and in the Aftermath of Armed Conflict report says: "If a child under the age of 15 is considered too young to fight, then he or she must also be considered too young to be held criminally responsible for serious violations of IHL while associated with armed forces or armed groups."

"Children are often desired as recruits because they can be easily intimidated and indoctrinated. They lack the mental maturity and judgment to express consent or to fully understand the implications of their actions . . . and are pushed by their adult commanders into perpetrating atrocities," the report said.

That children should be held accountable for their crimes during conflicts was acknowledged by the report, but "more effective and appropriate methods, other than detention and prosecution are encouraged, enabling children to come to terms with their past and the acts they committed."

The report said child soldiers should not be prosecuted "simply for association with an armed group or for having participated in hostilities . . . There are instances where children are accused of crimes under national or international law and are prosecuted before a criminal court. Prosecution of a child should always be regarded as a measure of last resort and the purpose of any sentence should be to rehabilitate and reintegrate the child into society."

Victims and Perpetrators

The International Criminal Tribunal for the former Yugoslavia (ICTY) and International Criminal Tribunal for Rwanda (ICTR) did not cite a minimum age for criminal responsibility, but no one under 18 appeared before the tribunals. The Statute of the Special Court for Sierra Leone (SCSL) provided the court with jurisdiction over any person above 15, but the court's prosecutor decided against indicting children for war crimes because of their dual status as both victims and perpetrators.

It may appear a grey area easily resolved by providing indemnity for crimes committed by child soldiers under the age of 15, but Radhika Coomaraswamy, SRSG for children and armed conflict, noted—in a 2010 article for the International Journal of Children's Rights: The Optional Protocol to the Convention on the Rights of the Child on the Involvement of Children in Armed Conflict—Towards Universal Ratification—that such a provision could be perversely used.

"If minor children who have committed serious war crimes are not prosecuted, this could be an incentive for their commanders to delegate to them the dirtiest orders, aiming at impunity. For this reason the ICC and SCSL focus strongly on those persons most responsible for human rights and IHL violations and apply the concept of command responsibility to political and military leaders," Coomaraswamy said.

Command responsibility does not necessarily remove individual culpability for serious human rights violations by lower ranks or subordinates, but "rather it traces liability back up the chain of command," said legal adviser to the ICRC Young.

When Child Soldiers Become Adults

Dominic Ongwen was about 10 when he became a soldier with the Lord's Resistance Army in the 1980s.

The ICC issued an arrest warrant for him in October 2005 for crimes against humanity, including enslavement of children. However, jurisdiction by the court does not extend to crimes committed by people under 18, and before 2002 when the Rome Statute entered into force. The crimes cited are for when Ongwen was an adult.

"Ongwen is the first known person to be charged with the same war crimes of which he is also a victim," the Justice and Reconciliation Project, a Ugandan NGO concerned with transitional justice, said in a 2008 field note entitled Complicating Victims and Perpetrators in Uganda: On Dominic Ongwen.

"[Ongwen and other child soldiers] represent precisely the kind of complex political victims who, if excluded from justice pursuits, could give birth to the next generation of perpetrators in Uganda; generations marginalized by the Judicial sector and who have nothing to gain from citizenship and nothing to lose from war," the field note observed.

The Lubanga Case

Tomaso Falchetta, Child Soldiers International (CSI) legal and policy adviser, told IRIN child soldiers should be viewed as victims and the NGO opposed their prosecution, as emphasis should be on the criminal responsibility of the adult recruiters. CSI "does not advocate for a cut-off point [for the prosecution of child soldiers], as it is a difficult issue."

The first person to stand trial at the ICC for enlisting children under 15 was former Democratic Republic of Congo (DRC) warlord Thomas Lubanga. His trial at The Hague is nearing completion after he allegedly recruited underage children into the Patriotic Forces for the Liberation of the Congo (FPLC) during the conflict in Ituri, a district in the eastern DRC, between 2002 and 2003.

An international humanitarian law expert, who declined to be identified, told IRIN Lubanga's case was "tremendously important" as "it will make others pause and think . . . Every rebel leader must be aware of this case."

Falchetta said it was "difficult to provide an empirical judgement on that [Lubanga's ICC prosecution being a deterrent]," and rather that accountability needed to be enforced at the national state level to discourage the continued use of child soldiers.

The former DRC president, Laurent Kabila, said in 2000 the armed forces would demobilize all child soldiers but a year after he made the commitment, four DRC child soldiers aged 14–16 were granted clemency, after death sentences imposed by a military tribunal led to international condemnation from human rights organizations. A 14-year-old child soldier was reportedly executed the previous year.

Capital punishment for persons under 18 violates the International Covenant on Civil and Political Rights and the Convention on the Rights of the Child. The DRC is party to both international human rights treaties.

"The DRC laws may be there [the use of child soldiers is illegal], but when it comes to implementation, investigation and prosecution [of adult recruiters], we've seen little of that," Falcetta said.

The CSI said in an April 2011 report (entitled Report to the Committee on the Rights of the Child in Advance of the DRC initial report on the Optional Protocol to the Convention on the Rights of the Child on the Involvement of Children in Armed Conflict) that "hundreds of children remain in the ranks of the national armed forces (Forces Armées de la Republique

"I Thomas Lubanga beg you to send me to prison instead."

Copyright © by Sneuro. Reproduction rights obtainable from www.CartoonStock.com.

Démocratique du Congo) despite legal and policy obligations to release them and government pledges to do so."

Laws of War

Matthew Happold of Hull University in the UK said in a 2005 paper entitled *The Age of Criminal Responsibility in International*

Criminal Law there were "good reasons" for regulating criminal responsibility of international crimes through international law as they were "often distinguished from crimes under national law because they transcend national boundaries and are of concern to the international community."

He said, in the paper presented at the Hague Academic Coalition's conference on international criminal responsibility, that from the perspective of a defendant, "it would seem wrong for an individual's liability under international law to depend upon the place of prosecution. . . . States are obliged to prosecute and punish offenders. Permitting States to decide their own age of criminal responsibility would allow them to determine the scope of their international obligations."

Child soldiers, like any other combatants are subjected to the Nuremburg principle that holds: "The fact that a person acted pursuant to order of his Government or of a superior does not relieve him from responsibility under international law, provided a moral choice was in fact possible to him."

ICC's Article 33 determines that acting on orders from superiors was not a defence of criminal responsibility but there are mitigating circumstances, and among them, is that a person may be relieved from prosecution if they did not know the order was unlawful.

However, the commission of "manifestly unlawful" crimes, such as genocide or crimes against humanity cannot be mitigated.

Young said the "so-called 'defence of superior orders' . . . the [Nuremberg] principle that 'I was just following orders' can no longer relieve any of us of criminal (and moral) responsibility for unconscionable acts we commit at the behest of others."

However, Rule 155 of Customary IHL, provided leeway, where "coercion and duress may provide exceptions . . . and one can quickly imagine how this principle might mitigate the responsibility of a child soldier who was forcibly recruited and forced, under threat of harm, to commit war crimes," ICRC adviser Young said.

ECOWAS Peacekeeping Efforts in Liberia Were Beneficial

Natalie E. Brown

Natalie E. Brown is deputy chief of mission at the US Embassy in Tunisia. In the following viewpoint, she says that the regional Economic Community of West African States (ECOWAS) was successful in creating a force to intervene in and help resolve the conflict in Liberia. However, she writes that the Liberian effort is not necessarily repeatable in other conflicts, and she suggests that ECOWAS should return to its original focus on economic and development issues rather than security.

In 1975 West African nations convened in Lagos and adopted the ECOWAS [Economic Community of West African States] Treaty to promote regional integration and establish an economic union of the area's Anglophone, Francophone, and Lusophone countries. ECOWAS has been moderately successful. It constructed highways, promoted anti-drug policies, and created a regional travelers' check, but the original goals remain elusive. Boundary disputes, periods of civil unrest in many of the countries, and enduring tensions between the French-speaking

Natalie E. Brown, "ECOWAS and the Liberia Experience: Peacekeeping and Self Preservation," US Department of State Report, 1999.

and English-speaking states impeded the formation of a real community.

The Success of ECOMOG

Despite its economic shortcomings, ECOWAS had one notable success. Its military arm, the Economic Community of West African States Military Observer Group (ECOMOG), restored peace and stability to Liberia. Liberia endured a violent, seven-year civil war as a result of a 1989 attempt by rebels to overthrow the government. Over the objections of some member states, ECOWAS created and deployed a military force to Liberia. The five-nation 3,500-person force that landed in Monrovia in 1990 would swell to a presence of more than 10,000 and represent the majority of the Community by 1996. Upon its 1998 departure, ECOMOG had negotiated peace accords and cease-fires, disarmed rebels, evacuated expatriates, and created conditions for transparent elections.

Buoyed by its success in Liberia, ECOWAS sent peacekeeping forces to other countries in turmoil. It further proposed the formation of a stand-by crisis response force and the creation of a permanent mechanism for conflict resolution. A cursory look at the experience suggests that West Africans were united in seeking to end the carnage. Stability and the humanitarian situation were concerns, but the participating states were motivated by their unique self-interests: domestic security, a desire to exert greater influence over the region, and pursuit of a better standing in the international community.

Despite its success in restoring peace to Liberia, ECOWAS is an economic body, not a military force. West Africa's fragility makes conflict resolution and mitigation a necessity. Nonetheless, ECOWAS should lessen its focus on forming a permanent mechanism to manage disputes and raising a regional army, and instead return to its original mission of economic development and integration to alleviate the economic and social tensions that fuel instability.

Welcome to West Africa

Mere mention of the region West Africa evokes images of civil unrest, refugees, famine, drought, pestilence, and corrupt military dictators living lavish lives at the expense of their countries and citizens. A still widely circulated 1994 article by Robert D. Kaplan published in *The Atlantic Monthly* presents a very pessimistic view of this African subregion, which he describes as "*the* [sic] symbol of worldwide demographic, environmental, and societal stress, in which criminal anarchy emerges as the real 'strategic' danger." To illustrate his point, he wrote of extortion by government officials, the need to hire armed bodyguards for a simple night out on the town, and mob violence carried out by all levels of society. According to Kaplan, West Africa is home to some of the "unsafest" places in the world.

Regrettably, many of the images described by Kaplan are accurate. Civil unrest is a constant threat to West African governments. Poverty is prevalent, and coupled with high population growth rates, will remain an obstacle to modernization and development. Diseases such as malaria and tuberculosis although treated in other parts of the world, go undiagnosed or ignored, and claim countless numbers each year. These are the realities of West Africa and they remain difficult to correct in the short-term due to the political, social, and economic underdevelopment of the region.

In spite of these depressing, harsh conditions, there are glimmers of hope. Democratization is spreading, economies are slowly growing, and African leaders are taking the initiative to resolve conflicts on the continent. One of the most notable examples of this new direction for Africa is the 1990–1997 West African peacekeeping and humanitarian operation in Liberia. Member nations of the Economic Community of West African States (ECOWAS) temporarily set aside their differences and through military force, diplomatic pressure, and humanitarian assistance restored peace and stability to war-torn Liberia.

The Limitations of ECOWAS

Buoyed by their success in Liberia, ECOWAS nations have since intervened in Sierra Leone and Guinea-Bissau, and further proposed the establishment of a regional military force and a permanent conflict mitigation body, the Mechanism for the Prevention, Management, Resolution of Conflicts, Peace-keeping [sic] and Security. While the ECOWAS success is a remarkable accomplishment for an area known for strife, in seeking to build on the Liberia success, ECOWAS states appear to have overlooked two important factors: 1) ECOWAS is not a peacemaking body, and 2) selfishness, not selflessness drove regional cooperation. The fundamental objectives of ECOWAS continue to be increased economic development and regional integration. The economic and social threats that growing chaos in Liberia posed to the greater region influenced the decision to intervene in Liberia and the creation of a military arm. Progress in developing a more economically sound western Africa may alleviate some of the conditions that gave rise to recent crises, and lessen the need for a full-time military force.

ECOWAS, in reflecting on the Liberia experience, also appears to have forgotten that there was no consensus on the decision to intervene. The West African nations had competing interests and what the organization achieved was more a result of the sixteen member states coming together to satisfy their individual needs than it was a manifestation of a shared desire to end the bloodshed. Self-preservation overruled any common commitment to peace, stability, or regional cooperation, although member states have convinced themselves otherwise.

Because of increased transnational threats to countries and regions, it may be necessary for ECOWAS states to maintain a military capability which can be tasked for specific circumstances. However, it is now premature for the region to construct a permanent peacekeeping mechanism and raise an armed force when the resources could be used to promote development and combat social problems. The Liberian experience offers valuable lessons for future peacekeeping activities. Nevertheless, the individual reasons of West African states involved that made the peacekeeping effort possible, and economic considerations may impede any systematic approach to conflict mitigation and management. . . .

Liberia's Ethnic Tensions

Chaos consumed Liberia for almost eight months before its neighboring states decided on, rather were forced into, active intervention. Liberia had a turbulent history, and in a region known for turmoil it was relatively easy for its neighbors to expect that Liberia's problems eventually would work themselves out. Liberia's fragility as a state emanated from its 1847 creation by freed American slaves. The founders, commonly known as America-Liberians, created a strict, hierarchical social system, placing themselves at the apex and the indigenous populations at the bottom. Although they only represented an approximate five percent of the population, for almost a century and a half they wielded political and economic control of the entire country.

The reign of the America-Liberians reached its culminating point during the 1971–1980 presidency of William Tolbert. Tolbert ascended to power following the death of President William Tubman, Liberia's strong man from 1944–1971. Tolbert was Tubman's vice president, and their combined thirty-six year rule brought only modest improvements to the lives of ordinary Liberians. Discontent flourished under Tolbert's reign, which was characterized by corruption and harassment. A crackdown on anti-Tolbert, America-Liberian elites and riots in 1979 over the price and availability [of] rice, a staple for all Liberians, further paved the way for political upheaval.

In 1980, Samuel Doe, a 28-year old Master Sergeant in the Liberian National Guard, led a coup d'état. Doe and his followers stormed the executive mansion, assassinated President Tolbert and his immediate security forces, and formed a revolutionary government. Subsequent executions of leading political figures and government officials effectively ended America-Liberian dominance. The Krahns, Doe's group and another ethic mi-

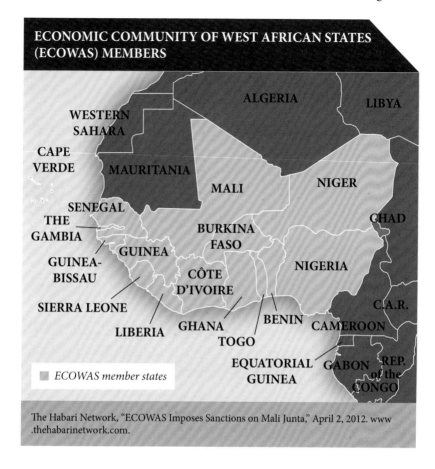

ECONOMIC COMMUNITY OF WEST AFRICAN STATES
(ECOWAS) MEMBERS

WESTERN
SAHARA

ALGERIA

LIBYA

CAPE
VERDE   MAURITANIA

MALI

NIGER

SENEGAL
THE
GAMBIA

BURKINA
FASO

CHAD

GUINEA

GUINEA-
BISSAU

CÔTE
D'IVOIRE

NIGERIA

SIERRA LEONE

LIBERIA   GHANA

BENIN   CAMEROON

C.A.R.

TOGO

EQUATORIAL   GABON   REP.
GUINEA   of the
CONGO

ECOWAS member states

The Habari Network, "ECOWAS Imposes Sanctions on Mali Junta," April 2, 2012. www
.thehabarinetwork.com.

nority, assumed the position once held by America-Liberians
in Liberia's social structure. Doe ruled with a heavy hand and
sanctioned Krahn violence against other ethnic groups as well
as against his detractors. Ethnic tensions along with government corruption and the economic and social problems common to developing African countries set the stage for a violent
reaction.

Such a response came in the form of Charles Taylor, an
America-Liberian, former official in the Doe Government, and
fugitive from justice in the United States. On December 24, 1989,
Taylor led a band of a few hundred rebels from a staging base
in Côte d'Ivoire across the border into Liberia with the aim of

ousting Doe and re-establishing Americo-Liberian supremacy. By late January 1990, Taylor's motley supporters had advanced from the border and seized Nimba County in north central Liberia, killing thousands of innocent civilians and forcing even more to seek refuge in nearby Côte d'Ivoire, Sierra Leone, and Guinea. Taylor and his supporters, calling themselves the National Patriotic Front of Liberia (NPFL), reached the capital city of Monrovia in June of the same year. The NPFL failed to force Doe out of the presidency and a standoff between Taylor, an NPFL splinter group, and the remains of the Liberian army ensued. A full-scale war involving numerous rebel groups and factions developed, tearing apart the country and its people for seven years.

West Africa to the Rescue

Initially, international response to the crisis in Liberia was muted. In 1990, the Iraqi invasion of Kuwait and the subsequent Gulf War captured headlines. Both the United States and the United Nations declined to intervene in restoring security to Liberia, advocating "African solutions to African problems." West Africa was on its own. Individual states and various African leaders, in the early days of the conflict, invoked regional agreements, appealing for but never achieving a cease-fire or negotiated settlement. This approach conformed to standing African prac-tices. Negotiation, mediation, conciliation, and arbitration were the preferred means for the peaceful resolution of conflicts and were in accordance with the 1963 Organization of African Unity (OAU) Charter. The OAU Charter served as guidance for the ECOWAS treaty which decreed:

- Non-aggression between Member States.
- Maintenance of regional peace, stability and security through the promotion and strengthening of good neighborliness.
- Peaceful settlement of disputes among Member States,

active co-operation between neighboring countries, and promotion of a peaceful environment.

These non-violent methods failed in Liberia, and by May 1990 its neighbors were desperate. The fighting affected regional trade and tourism, produced hundreds of thousands of refugees, and threatened to spill over into the border states. Under extreme pressure from Guinea and Sierra Leone, ECOWAS heads of states formed a five-member Standing Mediation Committee (SMC) comprised of representatives from the Gambia, Ghana, Mali, Nigeria, and Togo, and tasked it to identify a peaceful solution to the crisis. The Committee's initial attempts to negotiate a cease-fire were thwarted by Doe's refusal to step down. Other tactics, such as imposing travel restrictions, freezing assets located outside of Liberia, and restricting rebel use of sovereign territories for training fighters and for staging bases, were equally useless. Taylor and the emerging rebel factions were more interested in gaining ground and political power than in negotiating a solution to the conflict. When the SMC failed to forge a peace settlement, ECOWAS reluctantly concluded intervention was necessary.

Reluctant Intervention

Despite some opposition to intervention, during a two-day meeting in July 1990 in Sierra Leone, the ECOWAS sub-committee on Defense drew up a plan for a military intervention force. The SMC states met again in August and adopted the "ECOWAS Peace Plan for Liberia" which ordered the formation of the ECOWAS Monitoring Group in Liberia (ECOMOG). On August 23, 1990, only a few weeks later, 3,500 troops from Nigeria, Ghana, Guinea, Sierra Leone, and Gambia deployed to Liberia. Their mission was peacekeeping and humanitarian assistance and their tasks included:

- Imposition of a cease-fire.
- Disarmament of the warring parties.
- Ending the carnage of civilians.

- Imposition of an embargo on the acquisition and import of arms.
- Establishment of an interim government and preparation for elections.
- Evacuation of foreign nationals.

ECOMOG forces immediately seized the capital Monrovia and were able to enforce a temporary cease-fire. Taylor, angered by what he considered to be an attack on Liberia's sovereignty, led his rebels in a violent counter-attack. ECOMOG, in defending itself, changed from a humanitarian body into a political-military force. This new role became even more apparent when regional peacekeepers went on the offensive following the capture of Doe outside of ECOMOG headquarters by a rebel group. The transformation was complete after ECOMOG helped to install an interim government in Monrovia. Simultaneously, Taylor formed his own "government" in Gbarnga. These two acts effectively divided Liberia and forced ECOMOG to choose sides. As the only protector of the interim government and the opportunity for peace that it offered, ECOMOG forces had no option but to remain in Liberia as peacemakers, not peacekeepers.

For the next seven years, ECOMOG was the only source of stability in Liberia. Ironically, there was little concert within the peacemaking force and its regional sponsor, as member states debated the mandate and management of the force. Yet, as the conflict persisted, the ECOMOG presence enlarged. At its peak, the combined West African force comprised more than 10,000 troops, and included soldiers from the first five countries to deploy as well as from Mali, Burkina Faso, Niger, Senegal, and Benin. Côte d'Ivoire contributed a medical team, and some of the smaller states made modest financial contributions. As the civil war endured and the force size grew, ECOMOG's role and mission also changed. Observers reported as many as three distinct ECOMOGs during the Liberian conflict. The ECOMOGs varied according to the character traits of the force commanders and the political will of West African heads of state. In the early years of the war, ECOWAS believed a solution was on the horizon and assertively pursued peacekeeping activities. By the mid-nineties, rebels considered ECOMOG to be a party to the conflict, as self-defense and the protection of Monrovia and environs had become priorities for the West African mission. Traditional peacekeeping, peace enforcement, humanitarian assistance, and disarmament characterized the last years of the war. Additionally, by 1995 ECOMOG had also assumed the onerous task of protecting some 160 United Nations Observer Mission in Liberia (UNOMIL) observers. Despite ECOMOG's multiple personalities and ever changing responsibilities, the body would facilitate thirteen peace agreements, oversee the disarmament of 24,000 combatants, create a safe environment for transparent elections, distribute ballot boxes and other election materials; and provide security for the July 1997 presidential and national elections. . . .

The ECOWAS Identity Crisis

West Africa did a good thing and the region deserves international praise and gratitude. The countries worked through ideological differences, conflicts of interests, and rivalries, and also risked Nigerian dominion of the region to restore peace to Liberia. Nigerians were the most visible element of the peacekeeping force, but ECOMOG was a regional effort. ECOWAS members deployed what troops they could, contributed financially when possible, and offered their capitals for negotiations. To maintain the regional character of the operation, Mali, the Gambia, Togo, Côte d'Ivoire, Ghana, and Nigeria all hosted ECOWAS conferences, or meetings with Taylor or other faction leaders. This type of cooperation is unprecedented on the African continent. The Community demonstrated that regional cooperation is possible and very necessary.

The peacekeeping operation in Liberia and the proposal for a permanent apparatus for conflict mitigation indicate a regional political will to combat threats to stability. The impetuses to take action, however, were unique to each country. Selfishness propelled ECOWAS members to join ECOMOG and surprisingly enabled member states to work together. These same self-interests have prevented the countries from doing more as a region and will undermine a permanent peacekeeping organization. Rivalries will resurface, and there will only be consensus on how to manage Nigeria. Nigeria will undoubtedly be the most influential element of any peacekeeping or peacemaking effort. Its material and financial strength will translate into political weight, making it extremely difficult to effect an operation that goes against Nigerian will. A permanent structure also complicates both the decisions to intervene and to avoid a conflict. Both courses are ripe for accusations of bias based on language, ethnicity, or other social and political divisions.

The regional and international focus on peacekeeping has detracted from the original ECOWAS mission. For instance, Western donors have engaged many of the West African nations in peacekeeping and military capacity-building exercises, and the OAU has proposed raising subregional armies modeled on ECOMOG. Underdevelopment, sluggish economic growth, budget deficits, high debt service, and poor infrastructure make an ideal environment for breeding instability. For example, an electricity shortage during the spring and summer of 1998 created tense situations, as West African governments accused each other of willfully severing the flow of electricity through the region and demanding hard currency payment in advance for electrical services. Economic security will alleviate some of the tensions and facilitate future peace-promoting activities. Undersecretary of State for Political Affairs, Thomas Pickering, emphasized this basic need when he cautioned ECOWAS foreign ministers, "In the end, only economic growth will ensure lasting stability in West Africa."

Focus on Development

Economic growth will promote a more secure environment. It will also better prepare West Africa to respond to crises. ECOMOG may have noble intentions in establishing a permanent peace-keeping mechanism, but it currently lacks the necessary resources. Nigeria contributed significantly to the ECOMOG budget and there were small contributions from countries that did not provide troops to the operation. Despite the region's efforts, donor support from the West in the form of direct contributions, debt forgiveness, balance of payment support, and material and other transportation assistance sustained the peacekeeping mission. As recent as 1997, at the peak of the ECOWAS success as a peacekeeping body, member states were 45.5 million dollars in arrears to an organization whose annual budget is less than 10 million dollars. If member states cannot make their annual contributions to an organization designed to advance economic and social growth, the Community will be woefully unprepared to respond to future turmoil.

Historically, West Africa is the most fragile region on the African Continent. There will be strife, humanitarian crises, environmental disasters, and political instability. It is highly probable that ECOWAS, with one success under its belt, will have to raise a force and intervene again to restore security. The likelihood of peace or security operations in the future does not justify the exclusive focus on conflict management. ECOWAS should redirect its efforts and concentrate on attaining the goals it set twenty-five years ago. As a community, ECOWAS states have very little to unify them. A stake in the region's future through greater economic integration will pave the way for future cooperation in peace and stability and beyond. ECOWAS recognized this need when developing its long-term security program: "Economic Development can be more effectively pursued in an atmosphere of greater security . . . [and] effective economic integration and development is essential for security." ECOWAS should heed its own advice.

ECOWAS Peacekeeping Efforts Prolonged the Liberian Conflict

Luca Renda

Luca Renda is the country director for the United Nations Development Program in Lebanon. In the following viewpoint, he argues that the armed force of ECOWAS, called the Economic Community of West African States Monitoring Group (ECOMOG), did not reduce violence in the Liberian Civil War. Rather, he argues, ECOMOG prolonged the war, resulting in many more deaths than would have resulted if ECOMOG had stayed out of the conflict. Renda concludes that ECOMOG was essentially a tool of Nigerian foreign policy, designed to prevent Charles Taylor from gaining power in Liberia. As such, it was a participant in the war, rather than a peacekeeping force trying to end it.

Since Taylor's initial invasion, international actors played a significant role in the Liberian civil war. The Ivory Coast, Burkina Faso and Libya supported [Charles] Taylor. The Ivory Coast's President [Félix] Houphuet-Boigny was motivated by two main objectives: to get rid of Samuel Doe, and to replace him with a protégé under Ivorian influence so as to counter Nigerian designs on regional hegemony. Houphuet-Boigny introduced

Luca Renda, "Ending Civil Wars: The Case of Liberia," *The Fletcher Forum of World Affairs*, vol. 23, no. 2, 1999, pp. 66–71. Reproduced with permission.

Taylor to President Blaise Campaoré of Burkina Faso, who agreed to provide troops and transport facilities for the weapons. He also introduced Taylor to Moammar Gadhafi [President of Libya], who for a certain time provided training and weapons for NPFL [National Patriotic Front of Liberia] troops. Gadhafi's motivations are difficult to assess. He probably wanted to extend his influence in Sub-Saharan Africa or help overthrow Doe's regime, which had close ties to the United States. However, Houphuet-Boigny's support was indispensable to Taylor's NPFL.

International Factors in the Liberian War

Nigeria's President Ibrahim Babangida viewed the cooperation between Taylor and these three countries with apprehension. He saw it as a coalition against Nigeria and, as such, a potential source of regional destabilization. Nigeria was key to the creation of ECOMOG [Economic Community of West African States Monitoring Group], and throughout the war ECOMOG remained essentially an instrument of Nigerian foreign policy. This will be discussed further in a later section.

The United States had important interests in Liberia during the Cold War. Besides being the destination of substantial American investment, Liberia hosted American airfields, seaplane bases and telecommunication facilities. Because President Tolbert had adopted a policy of distancing himself from Washington, it was natural for the United States to initially support Doe after his coup. Doe soon realized that American support was vital, and between 1980 and 1985 Liberia became Africa's largest recipient of U.S. aid. However, Doe's abysmal record of human rights violations eventually raised protests in the U.S. Congress, and American support gradually declined. Despite that, in 1989 Doe was probably counting on American aid, which may have been a crucial factor in his decision to crush Taylor's invasion. Instead, the United States deliberately avoided any form of direct intervention in the crisis; it is almost certain that Charles Taylor had been informed of that decision.

It is difficult to assess relations between Taylor and the United States. In the earlier phases of the war, the U.S. government was exchanging intelligence reports with Taylor, which suggests that at least initially the United States did not see Taylor as an enemy. However, the U.S. attitude shifted and the United States firmly opposed Taylor through the duration of the conflict.

Analysis of ECOMOG Intervention

ECOMOG intervention was the first peacekeeping/peace-enforcing operation carried out independently by a regional organization ECOWAS [Economic Community of West African States], and is now widely viewed as a success. However, a closer analysis of this operation casts serious doubts on such a positive assessment. While ECOMOG's operations eventually did put an end to the Liberian war, the cost of this intervention was quite high. Between ECOMOG's intervention in 1990 to the end of the war in 1997, the estimated number of casualties rose from more than 4,000 to more than 150,000, and over one million people were displaced. Yet, the rapidity of Taylor's advance in 1989–1990 suggests that, in the absence of ECOMOG intervention, the NPFL leader would have probably succeeded in taking power within a year. This is not to say that violent fighting would not have taken place in Monrovia between NPFL and Doe's troops, or that a Taylor victory in 1990 would have created a democratic Liberia. But it is hard to imagine that the number of victims could have reached such a catastrophic figure without ECOMOG's intervention.

Nigeria and the other Anglophone countries justified the creation of ECOMOG on two main grounds. The first was that Article 18 of the ECOWAS Protocol of Mutual Assistance on Defense, signed in 1981, allowed for military intervention in a civil conflict, although only if "engineered and supported actively from outside." The argument was firmly contested by the Ivory Coast and Burkina Faso, which opposed the creation of ECOMOG since they supported Charles Taylor. Both countries questioned the real motives for the entire operation. In fact, the decision to establish ECOMOG was taken by the Standing Mediation Committee, which included only four members (Nigeria, Ghana, Gambia and Togo), and not by a full summit of ECOWAS member-states. ECOMOG's creation was further justified on humanitarian and regional security grounds. Nigeria's President [Ibrahim Badamasi] Babangida stated that the situation in Liberia had reached an intolerable level of brutality, and that refugee movement and spill-over of the war to neighboring countries were potential causes of regional instability.

Political Problems: Nigeria's Domination and the Lack of Internal Consensus

Since the very beginning, ECOMOG operations were constrained by deep divisions within ECOWAS. ECOMOG was essentially an operation initiated and dominated by Nigeria, whose aims were diametrically opposed to the interests of the Ivory Coast and Burkina Faso. Nigeria wanted to stop Taylor for two reasons. First, President Babangida enjoyed close relations with Doe and was interested in saving his presidency. Second and more importantly, Babangida had been informed that dissidents from Nigeria, Gambia, Guinea and Sierra Leone had trained in Libya with NPFL forces under the understanding that if Taylor succeeded, he would support them in similar insurrections in their own countries. According to Nigerian authorities, the NPFL was planning to destabilize the entire region.

The lack of internal consensus inside ECOWAS influenced the course of the operation and undermined most of the peace accords. Differences between ECOWAS members could be noticed as early as 1991 in the series of talks hosted by the Ivorian President Houphouet-Boigny. These meetings were perceived to be attempts to hijack Nigeria's peacekeeping efforts. They also signaled the intention of Taylor's main supporters to be in charge of the peace process. Following the signing of the Yamassourko IV agreement, Senegal agreed to contribute a sizeable contingent to ECOMOG's forces. This was important, as it introduced the first significant Francophone contingent in ECOMOG and served to broaden the base of support for the operation. However, Senegal from the outset distrusted Nigeria's leadership. When six Senegalese soldiers were killed in an encounter with NPFL soldiers, the entire contingent was withdrawn back to Monrovia, and within a year all Senegalese troops were removed from Liberia. In 1994 it was Ghana's President Jerry Rawlings' turn to take the initiative. In a move aimed at increasing his international status, Rawlings held secret meetings with Taylor. This resulted in a new round of meetings and peace agreements, which made ample concessions to Taylor and were therefore regarded suspiciously by Nigeria.

It was only after the collapse of those agreements that ECOWAS countries managed to achieve a certain degree of consensus. The Ivory Coast and Burkina Faso had ceased to support the NPFL, and since 1994, they had denied Taylor access to supply routes. Moreover, the new Nigerian government of Sani Abacha had reversed the strategy of combating Taylor, and the two leaders had held several meetings in 1995. These changes paved the way for the August 1995 signing of the Abuja agreement, which, for the first time, contained provisions to include members of the major warring factions in the collective presidency and allowed Taylor to peacefully enter Monrovia after six years of fighting. Subsequent problems further complicated the peace process, but at least from that moment, ECOWAS countries were able to provide a united front.

The Question of Neutrality

Despite ECOMOG's initial peacekeeping mandate, Taylor never viewed ECOMOG as neutral. Taylor was averse to any project involving external military intervention. The fact that 70 percent of ECOMOG's troops were Nigerian further aggravated the NPFL leader. After Doe's assassination, the relationship between Taylor and ECOMOG deteriorated. At the same time, the responsibili-

Fighting resumed in January 1996 near Monrovia after a breakdown in agreements brokered by ECOWAS. A cannon of the peacekeeping forces lies destroyed on the road as a Krahn member of the United Liberation Movement of Liberia (ULIMO) with a grenade launcher walks by. © AP Photo/Jean-Marc Bouju.

ties of ECOMOG soon expanded to include the enforcement of the peace agreements and its troops increased to more than 7,000. Nigeria provided most of the troops and heavy artillery. The situation became particularly tense after Taylor's failed Operation Octopus. ECOMOG responded with a full-scale offensive involving use of air and naval power, which resulted in thousands of casualties. ECOMOG was severely criticized for killing civilians, attacking relief convoys and violating Ivorian territory.

The most controversial element in ECOMOG's strategy against Taylor was its collusion with other factions. There is strong evidence that ECOMOG provided ULIMO [United Liberation Movement of Liberia for Democracy] (and subsequently the two ULIMO wings) and LPC [Liberia Peace Council] with arms, ammunition, transport and free passage to help press the war against Taylor. Assistance came also from individual ECOWAS member states. Guinea supported the mostly Mandingo ULIMO-K [K for its leader, Alhaji G.V. Kromah], whereas Nigeria first supported ULIMO-K and later switched to ULIMO-J [an ethnic Krahn faction led by General Roosevelt Johnson]. These factions provided ECOMOG with information on Liberia's topography, terrain, languages and customs. Personal economic interests were also involved. ECOMOG officers constantly engaged in illegal trafficking of looted goods with the factions through controlled ports and airfields.

The military and economic cooperation between ECOMOG and the factions hampered ECOMOG's ability to facilitate a resolution to the conflict particularly in the disarmament process. None of the faction leaders could trust ECOMOG as long as its commanders and soldiers had a personal stake in business deals with the various Liberian factions. More importantly, ECOMOG eventually lost control of its allied factions. Attracted by the huge profits of war, the factions started to operate independently and prolonged the conflict by undermining all peace agreements. When ECOMOG finally reached a peace settlement with Taylor in 1995, the factions opposed ECOMOG.

Mediation and Enforcement Capacity

In addition to the lack of internal consensus within ECOMOG and its cooperation with anti-Taylor factions, other factors contributed to weaken ECOMOG's capacity to serve as an effective mediator. Principally, ECOMOG had become a major participant in the conflict. At least until 1995, the Liberian conflict was essentially a war between Taylor and Nigeria, during which both sides sought but failed to impose a unilateral solution. This eventually resulted in a "mutually hurting stalemate" which paved the way for an agreement. For a long time, however, because the balance of power continuously fluctuated throughout the conflict, neither side felt motivated to enter serious negotiations.

In addition from the outset of the conflict, ECOMOG suffered from the inadequacy of its mandate, which probably resulted from a poor understanding of the situation on the ground. The operation was initially conceived as a traditional peacekeeping mission: just 2,000 troops, with the tasks of "monitoring ceasefires, restoring law and order and creating the necessary conditions for free and fair elections." But, there was no peace to keep, no ceasefire to monitor; and the entire operation had been undertaken without the consent of the main faction involved in the conflict—the NPFL. It is very likely that ECOMOG planners had grossly underestimated the military potential of Taylor's forces, as well as their capacity to sustain themselves economically. This initial mistake played a crucial role because it led to the further escalation of the conflict.

As a would-be mediator, ECOWAS had the responsibility of making credible proposals. Yet, with the arguable exception of the Cotonou Accord, all peace agreements were generally poorly drafted, simplistic and characterized by unrealistic timetables. They failed to address the complexity of Liberia's conflict, and particularly the problems related to the material benefits the parties extracted from the war. ECOWAS' approach toward Taylor was especially counterproductive. Throughout the conflict, Taylor agreed to negotiate only under intense military or diplomatic pressure. On those occasions, ECOWAS repeatedly made concessions to the NPFL leader by acceding to most of his demands. This strategy sent the wrong signals to Taylor, who exploited every truce to reorganize his troops and renew his attacks.

New problems arose after Nigeria and NPFL eventually came to an agreement in 1995. The provision of the Abuja Accord to allocate to faction leaders the control of executive positions (especially the government economic agencies) led to appointments based not on merit, but rather on factional and ethnic affiliation.

Negotiations were further complicated by the proliferation of factions caused by ECOMOG policy. In fact, a major flaw in the Abuja Accord was the exclusion of Roosevelt Johnson, leader of ULIMO-J, from the Council of State, due to behind-the-scenes maneuvering by Charles Taylor and Alhaji Kromah. This altered the balance of power among the factions and eventually led to a new outbreak of fighting in Monrovia in April 1996.

ECOMOG's enforcement capacity was constantly undermined by the lack of adequate resources and problems related to the multinational composition of the mission, which caused serious difficulties in command and control. The exact cost of the operation is unknown, but estimates put the figure at around U.S.$2 billion. Nigeria shouldered at least 70 percent of the financial burden, and provided the fuel for the entire operation, together with most of the heavy weaponry, military aircraft and naval vessels. The United States provided regular financial assistance to the operation, but this amounted to a meager U.S.$10 million a year and was largely insufficient. Until 1996, financial constraints played an especially critical role in undermining the creation of a comprehensive disarmament program, as they made it extremely difficult to provide the combatants with a credible economic alternative to fighting.

ECOMOG's Failures

ECOMOG failed to satisfy the main requirements for a successful conflict resolution effort. In terms of timeliness, the intervention was launched when the conflict was not ripe for resolution. As a peacekeeping mission, it was ill conceived because there was no peace to keep, and it lacked the consent of a major faction, NPFL. As a peace enforcement operation, it was ill equipped to impose a unilateral solution to the conflict. Problems of internal consensus affected the coordination among ECOWAS countries, which were driven by strategic and economic interests. Finally, because of its controversial relations with the warring factions, ECOMOG failed to establish a climate of trust among the factions.

Refugees, Such as Those from Liberia, Tend to Spread Conflict and Violence

Sarah Kenyon Lischer

Sarah Kenyon Lischer is an associate professor of political science at Wake Forest University in Winston-Salem, North Carolina. In the following viewpoint, she argues that humanitarian aid during refugee crises often ends up prolonging military conflict and aiding combatants. She says refugee camps become staging grounds for military action and aid often ends up feeding combatants. In Liberia, she notes, rebel groups systematically stole equipment and supplies from humanitarian groups. She suggests that humanitarian groups need to confront the military and political results of aid.

After organizing the mass killing of hundreds of thousands of Rwandan Tutsi in 1994, the Rwandan Hutu leadership forced over a million Hutu civilians into eastern Congo (then Zaire). During the refugee crisis from 1994 to 1996, perpetrators of the Rwandan genocide established military training bases adjacent to the refugee camps. The militants stockpiled weapons, recruited and trained refugee fighters, and launched cross-border attacks against Rwanda. The militant leaders openly gloated about their manipulation of the Hutu refugees and their

Sarah Kenyon Lischer, *Dangerous Sanctuaries: Refugee Camps, Civil War, and the Dilemmas of Humanitarian Aid,* Cornell University Press, 2005, pp. 1–9. Reproduced with permission.

plan to complete the genocide of the Tutsi. From the camps, the genocidal leader Jean Bosco Barayagwiza boasted that "even if [the Tutsi-led Rwandan Patriotic Front] has won a military victory it will not have the power. We have the population." In late 1996, the growing strength of the militant groups provoked a Rwandan invasion and attacks against refugees. Until the fighting disrupted their operations, international humanitarian organizations regularly delivered food and supplies to military bases and refugee camps.

Refugees as a Cause of War

Eastern Congo became the epicenter of a regional war in which over a dozen states and rebel groups fought one another and plundered the region's resources. An estimated three million Congolese died as a result of this war, mostly from preventable diseases and malnutrition. A major cause of war was the internationally supported refugee population, which included tens of thousands of unrepentant perpetrators of genocide. Between 1994 and 1996, international donors spent billions of dollars to sustain that population. These same donors refused to fund efforts to disarm the militants or to send peacekeeping troops to do so.

Every year, millions of people flee their homes to escape violent conflict. Often the resulting refugee crisis leads to an expansion of violence rather than an escape. In some cases, refugee crises function as a strategy of war. For exiled rebel groups, a refugee population provides international legitimacy, a shield against attack, a pool of recruits, and valuable sources for food and medicine. In essence, refugee camps function as rear bases for rebels who attack across the border. Refugee sending states view refugees as an indictment of the government's legitimacy and as a potential military threat. The sending state may pursue refugees across the border, subjecting them to military attack. As cross-border attacks escalate, the risk of international war grows. Eventually, the entire region may be destabilized as more states are drawn in to the conflict.

The recurring pattern of violent refugee crises prompts the following questions: Under what conditions do refugee crises lead to the spread of civil war across borders? How can refugee relief organizations respond when militants use humanitarian assistance as a tool of war? What government actions can prevent or reduce the spread of conflict? . . .

The United States and the Militarization of Refugees

The spread of civil war due to refugee crises has occurred, or threatened to occur, numerous times throughout history and around the globe. One early attempt to militarize refugees occurred after World War II, when President [Dwight D.] Eisenhower pursued a plan to enlist stateless Europeans into the U.S. army as a covert anti-communist force. General Robert L. Cutler, special assistant to the president for national security, described Eisenhower's vision as an army of 250,000 "stateless, single, anti-Communist young men, coming from countries behind the iron curtain." Eventually the plan faltered because of European concerns about the divisive political implications of such a force.

In the decades after World War II, the great powers viewed refugees as political actors and often abetted their militarization. Looking back on the Cold War period, Myron Weiner commented: "Since refugees were often regarded as part of an armed struggle in the cold war the question of demilitarizing camps did not arise. . . . It would not be too great an exaggeration to say that in many circumstances UNHCR [the UN Refugee agency] and NGOs [non-governmental organizations] were instruments of the United States and its allies for coping with the humanitarian consequences of cold war conflicts." During the Cold War, refugee crises contributed to the spread of civil war in South and Southeast Asia, Central America, Southern Africa, and the Middle East.

The refugee crisis sparked by the Vietnamese invasion of Cambodia in 1979 created an internationally supported battleground on the Thai-Cambodian border. Hundreds of thousands

A man holds a bag of rice looted from a shipping container with food aid at a Monrovia, Liberia, port in August 2003. © Issouf Sanogo/AFP/Getty Images.

of refugees straddled the border in a series of camps that were controlled by the various Cambodian rebel groups, including the genocidal but anti-communist Khmer Rouge. The United States supported the anti-communist rebel groups despite the blatant military activity among the refugees and the misuse of humanitarian assistance. The United Nations provided assistance to the refugees but refused to offer legal or physical protection. One expert, Courtland Robinson, convincingly argues that the international response needlessly prolonged the refugee crisis and revitalized the Khmer Rouge.

Cold War politics also affected Nicaraguan and Salvadoran refugees in Central America. During the 1980s at least 300,000 people from war-torn Nicaragua and El Salvador fled to Honduras. The United States supported the militant activities of the anti-communist *contra* rebels based among the Nicaraguan refugees, encouraging cross-border attacks against the sending state. In the UNHCR-assisted camps, "contras were also apparently free to come and go and used the camps for rest, political and logistical support, and recruitment." In contrast, Salvadoran refugees, perceived as enemies of the right-wing government in El Salvador, suffered oppression and attacks at the hands of Honduran and Salvadoran government forces.

Africa and Palestine

In Africa, international agencies supported refugees who sought to topple white dominated governments in South Africa, Zimbabwe, and Namibia. The regional conflict spread as the South African government retaliated with bombing raids against refugee settlements in Angola, Botswana, and other border states, killing hundreds of civilians (as well as some rebels). Donors generally viewed those refugees as victims—rather than perpetrators—of violence and regarded their struggles against apartheid as legitimate.

One of the most enduring and violent situations involves the millions of Palestinian refugees scattered throughout the Middle East. These refugees have been involved in the spread of conflict in Jordan, Lebanon, and the West Bank and the Gaza Strip. In the 1970s the refugees precipitated civil war in Jordan. In the 1980s Israeli-backed forces in Lebanon massacred thousands of refugees as part of a crackdown on militant Palestinian groups. Battles between Palestinian militants and Israeli security forces have raged in the refugee camps of the West Bank and the Gaza Strip. Such a highly politicized and militarized environment has eroded the neutrality of humanitarian organizations. For example, Israel has accused the United Nations Relief and Works

Agency (UNRWA), formed specifically to assist the Palestinians, of politicizing its aid work and supporting militant elements.

Since the early 1990s, refugee crises in Central Africa, the Balkans, West Africa, and the Middle East have led to the international spread of internal conflict. In 2001, a United States government analysis reckoned, "the recent military interventions in Fiji and Côte d'Ivoire; ethnic conflicts in the former Yugoslavia, the former Soviet Union, eastern Indonesia, and Democratic Republic of the Congo; and the Arab-Israeli dispute have resulted in part from large-scale migration and refugee flows." That analysis also predicted that migration to less-developed countries would continue to "upset ethnic balances and contribute to conflict or violent regime change."

The humanitarian fiasco in eastern Congo kindled an awareness of the military and political implications of refugee crises. Freed from Cold War politics, policymakers are now more receptive to the idea of reducing military activity affecting refugees. At the same time, however, the great powers have generally lost strategic interest in developing countries and are unwilling to commit resources to demilitarize refugee areas. As the United States, Russia, and the former colonial powers disengage from many conflicts in the developing world, humanitarian agencies often remain the only international presence during a refugee crisis.

Status Quo Policy: Ignoring Militarization

"Why should UNHCR be worried about weapons?"
—UNHCR protection officer, Geneva, July 1998.

Despite the political and military implications of refugee crises, the international response to a crisis usually consists of humanitarian assistance. Both governments and humanitarian organizations pay little attention to the politics of the refugee crisis or the conflict that created the displacement, instead, private charities, UN organizations, and the Red Cross expertly provide food, shelter, health care, and sanitation facilities for the refugees. Western governments often fund international humanitarian organizations as a substitute for political or military involvement. Such donor states generally do not view militarized refugee crises as a threat to national security.

When conflict escalates, governments and humanitarian organizations tend to blame each other. After the Rwandan refugee crisis in Zaire, politicians condemned aid workers for succoring genocidal killers. Aid agencies accused governments of abandoning humanitarians in a military and political quagmire. Yet during the crisis, both states and humanitarian organizations willfully ignored its political and military aspects.

Humanitarian organizations generally assess the political context of the crisis only insofar as it affects the delivery of aid. In many cases, aid agencies regard military activity that does not directly impinge on their activities among the refugees as irrelevant. Aid workers often ignore militarization as long as the weapons and military training remain out of sight—quite literally. During the late 1990s, for example, humanitarian officials conceded that Burundian rebels had mingled with the refugees in Tanzanian camps. Yet aid workers did not consider the camps militarized because the rebels conducted their military activities in the bush and on the Burundi border, evading direct observation. Because of that humanitarian myopia, militants can reap the benefits of international aid—as long as they maintain a low profile.

Practical reasons also encourage humanitarian organizations to ignore militarization. Legally, it is not aid agencies but the receiving state that must provide security in refugee crises. Without support from the receiving state, the unarmed humanitarians have little capacity to oppose military activity. Militarization condoned by the receiving state or a powerful donor state sharply limits the options humanitarian organizations can pursue.

Ethical issues cloud the issue of militarization as well. Humanitarian organizations express ambivalence about encouraging—or forcing—refugees to return home, even when it seems the only solution to militarization. The norm against *refoulement* (forced return) is deeply ingrained, both in the culture of humanitarian organizations and in international law. A second ethical qualm concerns the uneasy relationship between aid organizations and security organizations. Philosophically, many non-governmental organizations (NGOs) oppose the presence of armed guards or security details for humanitarian missions. Some NGOs view reliance on any form of coercion as antithetical to the humanitarian enterprise.

In situations where refugee crises are exploited as a strategy of war, the purely humanitarian response is not only inadequate, it can be counterproductive. Well-intentioned humanitarian assistance that ignores the existing political risk factors for militarization will end up exacerbating the conflict. Both states and aid organizations often operate under the mistaken assumption that humanitarian activity in the absence of military or political attention to the crisis is better than no action at all. In some instances, as in the Rwandan refugee crisis in Zaire, ignoring militarization while distributing aid did intensify the conflict. Neutral humanitarian action was not possible. In fact, the most helpful response to a potentially violent refugee crisis is a robust peace-enforcement mission with the aim of disarming militants and securing the refugee camps.

Following the debacle in the Rwandan refugee camps, a number of critics exposed the perverse effects of humanitarian aid. These scholars and NGO practitioners uncovered many of the negative effects of assistance during conflict and, in many cases, offered scathing critiques of the existing policies. It remains to be seen how these critiques will influence actual practice during refugee crises.

How Refugee Relief Exacerbates Conflict
"We are going to be feeding people who have been perpetrating genocide."

—Charles Tapp, chief executive of the charity CARE, quoted in *Rwanda: Death, Despair, and Defiance* (1995)

The Rwandan Genocide

The massacres in the Rwandan genocide were carried out in the open—roughly 800,000 Tutsi were killed in a hundred days. The state organized the killings, but the killers were, by and large, ordinary people. The killing was done mainly by machete-wielding mobs. People were killed by their neighbors and workmates, and even by human rights advocates and spouses.

Unlike Nazi Germany, where the authorities made every attempt to isolate victims from the general population, the Rwandan genocide was both a more public and a more intimate affair. Street corners, living rooms, and churches became places of death. It was carried out by hundreds of thousands of people, and witnessed by millions. In a private conversation with the author in 1997, a Rwandan government minister contrasted the two horrors. "In Germany," he said, "the Jews were taken out of their residences, moved to distant far away locations, and killed there, almost anonymously. In Rwanda, the government did not kill. It prepared the population, enraged it and enticed it. Your neighbors killed you" (Mamdani 2001, p. 6). A few years ago, four Rwandan civilians stood trial for crimes against humanity in Belgium. Among the four were two nuns and a physicist. The challenge for academic writing is to explain the perversely "popular" character of the violence.

Mahmood Mamdani, "Genocide in Rwanda," in
John Hartwell Moore, ed. Encyclopedia of
Race and Racism, *vol. 2, Detroit: Macmillan*
Reference USA, 2008, p. 52.

There are four main ways that humanitarian aid in refugee crises can exacerbate conflict: feeding militants, sustaining and protecting militants' dependents, supporting a war economy, and providing legitimacy to combatants. The optimal conditions for these mechanisms to thrive include a high level of political cohesion among the refugees and low state capability or willingness to provide security.

Feeding militants. At the most basic level, direct assistance to militants, both intentional and otherwise, relieves them of having to find food themselves. Inadvertent distribution occurs when militants hide among the refugees. For example, at the beginning of the Rwanda crisis in 1994, many aid workers were unaware of the genocide that had preceded it. Hutu militants implemented a successful propaganda effort painting the Hutu as victims and ignoring the genocide. David Rieff [writer] quotes an American engineer who arrived in Goma, in Zaire, technically prepared but politically ignorant: "I went to Goma and worked there for three solid months. But it was only later, when I finally went to Rwanda on a break, that I found out about the genocide, and realized, 'Hey, I've been busting my butt for a bunch of ax murderers!'"

In some cases, NGOs have intentionally provided food directly to militants. In the Zaire camps, some NGOs rationalized that if the Hutu militants did not receive aid, they would steal it from the refugees. Another rationale was strict adherence to the humanitarian imperative of impartiality—that is, providing assistance based on need—without determining if the recipients included hungry warriors. Fabrizio Hochschild, an official under the United Nations High Commissioner for Refugees, summed up this logic when he defended UNHCR action during the Rwanda crisis: "Even the guilty need to be fed."

Sustaining and protecting militants' dependents. Even if assistance does not directly sustain the militants, it can support their war aims by succoring their civilian families and supporters. Humanitarian assistance relieves militants from providing goods and services for their supporters. Rebels can live outside of the camps, while sending their families to the camps to live in relative safety. As a Sudanese refugee in the violence-plagued Ugandan camps confirmed, "the [Sudanese rebel] commanders keep their wives and families in the camps."

Ironically, militants often present themselves as a "state in exile," even though it is the humanitarian organizations that provide many of the functions of the state. As [writer] Mary Anderson explains, "When external aid agencies assume responsibility for civilian survival, warlords tend to define their responsibility and accountability only in terms of military control." By sustaining and protecting civilian dependents, aid organizations allow the militant leaders to focus on fighting rather than on providing for their supporters.

Supporting a war economy. Militants can use relief resources to finance conflict. It is not uncommon for refugee leaders to levy a war tax on the refugee population, commandeering a portion of all rations and salaries. Refugee leaders can also divert aid when they control the distribution process. During the Rwandan refugee crisis, militant leaders diverted large amounts of aid by inflating population numbers and pocketing the excess. Alain Destexhe, secretary general of Médecins Sans Frontières (Doctors Without Borders), in discussing Goma, in Zaire, noted that "food represents power, and camp leaders who control its distribution divert considerable quantities towards war preparations." A Liberian refugee in Guinea observed in 2002 that "The same food the UN is bringing here is being used for the war in Liberia."

Armed groups often raid warehouses and international compounds to steal food, medicine, and equipment. Thousands, if not millions, of dollars of relief resources, including vehicles and communication equipment, are stolen every year. In the mid-1990s, aid organizations curtailed their operations in Liberia after the theft of $20 million in equipment during the civil war there. The International Committee of the Red Cross reported that "the level of diversion by the factions had reached a systematic and planned level, that it was integrated into the war strategy. . . . It had become obvious that the factions were opening the doors to humanitarian aid, up to the point where all the sophisticated logistics had entered the zones: cars, radios, computers, telephones. When all the stuff was there, then the looting would start in a quite systematic way."

Defenders of aid organizations are quick to point out that, in many cases, humanitarian assistance forms a negligible part of the resources available to combatants. There are two responses to this argument. First, even a relatively small role does not absolve humanitarian organizations of responsibility. Absolute amounts matter as much as relative measures: The $20 million of equipment stolen in Liberia during the mid-1990s was $20 million that aid agencies could not use for other crises, regardless of the relative importance of aid resources in Liberia's conflict. Second, the nonmonetary benefits of humanitarian aid as a resource of war are also important. The legitimacy conferred by humanitarian activity can bolster the strength of a rebel group, regardless of the cash value of the aid.

Legitimacy

Providing legitimacy to combatants. Humanitarian assistance shapes international opinion about the actors in a crisis. To raise money from Western publics and governments, aid agencies tend to present oversimplified stories that emphasize the helplessness and victimization of the refugees. Aid to the Rwandan refugees established a perception of the Hutu refugees as needy victims, obscuring their role as perpetrators of genocide against the Tutsi.

Aid also provides international legitimation of a group's political goals. The ruling party in Angola, the Movimento Popular da Libertação de Angola (MPLA), repeatedly used humanitarian assistance to bolster its political standing during its civil war throughout the 1990s. One member of the opposition, the União Nacional para a Independência Total de Angola (UNITA), explained:

> The greatest problem is that people confuse humanitarian assistance as assistance from the MPLA party. The MPLA have taken advantage of this situation and many people think that what [aid] arrives has been given by the MPLA, not by the international aid organizations nor [sic] the government. . . . We don't have access to distribution of humanitarian aid, this

is going to affect with certainty the electoral constituency of the future.

Rebel groups also manipulate aid agencies to increase their legitimacy and profile in the international media. To gain access to a needy population, humanitarian agencies are often forced to negotiate with unsavory rebel or government groups. The very act of negotiation solidifies the reputation of such groups as powerful and legitimate.

Despite the proven political uses of humanitarian aid, many impassioned arguments suggest that impartiality and neutrality are both possible and desirable. Rieff makes a principled argument that humanitarianism "is neutral or it is nothing." More practically, aid workers fear becoming targets in the conflict and losing access to the needy population if combatants view their work as political. Advocates of strict neutrality rarely admit that by giving aid in a supposedly impartial and neutral manner, their actions may benefit one or more combatants and lead to further war. In reality, any humanitarian action in a conflict zone will have political, and possibly military, consequences no matter how apolitical the intent. Thus, in a militarized refugee crisis, humanitarian organizations may have to decide between aiding both killers and refugees and aiding no one at all.

Can Refugees Benefit the State? Refugee Resources and African Statebuilding

Karen Jacobson

Karen Jacobson is a visiting associate professor at the Fletcher School of Law and Diplomacy at Tufts University. In the following viewpoint, she argues that refugee camps can have a beneficial effect on host countries. She writes that humanitarian aid can benefit host economies, and often finds its way into the hands of locals as well as refugees. Further, she explains that refugees bring with them money, property, and skills that may benefit the host country. As an example she cites Liberian refugee entrepreneurs in Ghana who started businesses to build houses and deliver water. Jacobson concludes that refugees create problems, too, but that in some situations the advantages may outweigh the difficulties.

For the past thirty years or more, African countries have experienced repeated and sustained mass influxes of refugees. These influxes are widely seen as one more intractable problem—'a luxury [the world's poorest states] . . . can no longer afford' as a recent text put it (UNHCR 1998: 71). While refugees impose a variety of security, economic and environmental burdens on host

Karen Jacobson, "Can Refugees Benefit the State? Refugee Resources and African Statebuilding," *Journal of Modern African Studies,* vol. 40, no. 4, December 2002, pp. 577–586. Reproduced with permission.

countries, they also embody a significant flow of resources in the form of international humanitarian assistance, economic assets and human capital. Refugee camps become repositories of such resources as relief supplies and food aid, vehicles, communication equipment, employment and transport contracts with relief agencies, and other locally valued and scarce materials. The refugees themselves bring human capital in the form of labour, skills and entrepreneurship, and they are conduits for remittance flows. Since most refugee situations in Africa are protracted—refugees remain in host countries for many years—these resources are available to the host country for an extended period of time. In addition, refugees are, if only for a brief burst of international media attention, a highly visible phenomenon, capable of focusing attention on regions normally lost to the public eye. They therefore represent political leverage for savvy actors, including the state itself. . . .

Resources and Security Problems: The Double Impact of Refugee Flows

The belief that refugees impose significant economic and environmental burdens on their host communities is widely accepted and well documented. Every host country in Africa has its set of studies describing these burdens.[1] Host governments complain that refugees compete with locals for scarce resources such as land, jobs and environmental resources (e.g. water, rangeland or firewood), and overwhelm existing infrastructure such as schools, housing and health facilities. These concerns underpin the state's rationale for keeping refugees in camps, where they can be assisted and managed by international refugee agencies.

The counter-argument, presented below, is that the presence of refugees can increase the overall welfare of the host community in two ways: international refugee assistance 'trickles out' into the community, and the economic activities of refugees contribute to the host community's standard of living. . . .

International Refugee Assistance and the Host Community

Humanitarian assistance is of two main types: food aid, and non-food aid which includes material and personnel resources intended to provide for the medical, shelter, security, educational and repatriation/resettlement needs of refugees. International refugee assistance is provided in three ways: on a bilateral (inter-governmental) basis; through international organisations (primarily UNHCR); and by non-governmental organisations. Most assistance is channelled through UNHCR which makes arrangements with the host government and with implementing NGOs to provide for the refugees. It takes the form of in-kind contributions (food, medicine, tools, logistical personnel, aircraft etc.), or funds made available to purchase goods and services. . . .

Although international refugee assistance is usually intended for refugees in camps, it finds its way into the host community. Both food and non-food aid items are traded in local markets and further afield.[2] In addition, many international refugee agencies deliberately make relief assistance available to local people so as to increase the receptiveness of the host community to refugees. UNHCR's Handbook for Emergencies states that in situations where there are tensions between refugees and the local population, one of the measures to be considered is: 'Benefiting the local community through improvements in infrastructure in the areas of water, health, roads, etc.' This approach is embodied in UNHCR's Refugee Affected Areas programmes, which provide new or improved transport infrastructure (roads, bridges), health clinics and schools, both as an inducement to locals to assist refugees, and to improve the delivery of humanitarian assistance. Such programmes have been implemented in countries such as Zambia, Tanzania and Uganda. In Zambia, an initiative in Western Province, where there are at least 60,000 Angolan refugees, was launched to provide much needed transport, health and agricultural infrastructure. According to one informant[3]:

Part of the initiative was to induce the Litunga (chief of the Lozi people) to grant additional land for a new refugee camp. Part too, was because UNHCR and the implementing partners had great difficulty getting food and materials out to the camps because of the crummy roads and unreliable ferry over the Zambezi . . . The idea of getting money out of donors to improve the possibility of delivery of goods and services to refugees is, in the case of Zambia, a good one. It presents a win-win situation in which both local government and refugees profit.

In Uganda, an estimated 40% of the assistance provided by UNHCR in Kibanda district was directed to the area surrounding the refugee settlement at Kiryandongo, in order to mitigate possible resentment by the local population (Kaiser 2000: 7). In Tanzania's Kigoma and Kagera regions, the Special Programme for Refugee Affected Areas was a donor and government sponsored programme operating from the Prime Minister's Office. According to one observer, it represented 'a kind of wish list including all the development projects that the administration could not afford on its own' (Landau 2001). The line between humanitarian and development assistance is a thin one, and it is in the interests of all actors not to define it too clearly.[4]

Host communities also benefit when relief agencies allocate part of their humanitarian assistance budget to offset the negative impact of refugees, especially those associated with the environment and public health. Environmental problems occur when refugees rely on 'free' natural resources either to support themselves (construct housing or collect food and firewood) or to make a living. Economic activities like charcoal making, firewood and thatch grass selling, and the cultivation of hillsides, can overburden water supplies and range land, and local people resent this use of resources. In recent years, relief agencies have sought to offset these burdens. For example, in 1998, UNHCR took early protective measures in Tanzania's Kigoma region to prevent the kind of environmental degradation that occurred in Kagera with the Rwandan influx in 1994. In several countries, including northeastern Kenya (the Dadaab camp complex for Somali refugees), and the forest region of Guinea, UNHCR has made provision for environmental programmes, road and other infrastructural repair, supplemental health clinics and schools for local people, and so on. UNHCR and many NGOs advocate the integration of refugee services with national services (Sphere Project 1997; UNHCR 1999), and work with national ministries of health to build up local health services. This occurred in eastern Zaire during the refugee crisis of the 1990s (Goyens et al. 1996), and in Guinea, where the government and UNHCR agreed that refugees from Sierra Leone and Liberia could have access to national health services, with UNHCR covering the cost of the refugees' health care (Van Damme 1995).

The benefits of refugee assistance persist after refugees repatriate or are relocated, and resources such as buildings and transportation equipment are turned over to the local community. After the Mozambican repatriation from Malawi was completed in 1995, UNHCR handed over refugee facilities including schools, clinics and vehicles worth $35 million to the Malawi government, which also requested $78 million from UNHCR for reforestation to offset the deforestation resulting from the refugee presence (World Refugee Survey 1996: 57). Clean-up of camps and rehabilitation of the environment is usually funded by international agencies and implemented in cooperation with the local community. For example, in southern Guinea in late 2000, after Sierra Leonean refugees were relocated away from the border to escape rebel cross-border raids, the World Food Programme worked with locals to clean up some seventy-four former camps in the 'Parrot's Beak' area. A second phase of the project, launched in November 2001 and funded by the US government, involved rehabilitating the environment in refugee hosting areas, and promoting environmentally sound food security (IRIN 3.6.2002).[5]

In sum, although host communities may be burdened by an initial influx of refugees, there are also likely to be benefits in

UNITED NATIONS HIGH COMMISSIONER FOR REFUGEES (UNHCR) EXPENDITURES IN FY2000 ON KEY REFUGEE HOSTING COUNTRIES IN SUB-SAHARAN AFRICA	
Country	Amount (US $1,000)
Côte d'Ivoire	6,025
Sierra Leone	7,496
Angola	7,578
Somalia	8,001
Rwanda	10,074
Zambia	11,376
Sudan	13,881
Uganda	15,070
Liberia	16,484
Kenya	22,407
Guinea	26,972
Tanzania	29,707

Data from UNHCR 2002 Global Appeal, www.unhcr.ch/pubs.

Source: Karen Jacobson, "Can Refugees Benefit the State? Refugee Resources and African State Building," *Journal of Modern African Studies,* December 2002, vol. 40, no. 4, p. 581.

the form of infrastructural resources and funding for both the host population and the state that accrue from international refugee assistance. The presence of international relief agencies also provides resources like employment for locals, and transportation and other service contracts which benefit local operators. These benefits are often not immediately apparent, because they are phased over the course of the refugee stay, not during the emergency. Nor do they benefit everyone in the hosting area. As with any economic shift, poorer people in the community are more likely to come off badly. One of the most notorious ways in which relief agencies affect the local economy is through their impact on housing. The influx of international personnel drives up the price of housing and reduces availability, with negative consequences for the poor (of whom refugees are often a large proportion). Some dramatic examples of this occurred in Goma, during the 1994–96 Rwandan refugee crisis, and again in 2002, as well as in Freetown, Kigali, Nairobi, and other African cities. Whether refugee-generated resources and benefits are sufficient to balance the burden imposed by the refugees is an empirical question and must be decided on a case-by-case basis.

The Economic Contribution of Refugees to the Host Community

A second way in which the host country potentially benefits from protracted refugee situations is from the economic contribution made by refugees themselves. Refugees bring assets and resources, including social capital, into the host area. Assets include material goods brought with them from their home countries, ranging from gold to trucks to cattle and computers. Or over the course of time, refugees act as conduits for remittances from abroad—a key source of foreign exchange. In addition to the funds *per se,* the informal remittance industry in camps creates all kinds of spin-offs in the form of telephone companies, banks and courier services. Nairobi is a flourishing example of the remittance industry at work.

A key contribution of refugees is their entrepreneurship. In Buduburam, a Liberian refugee camp in Ghana, Shelley Dick (2002) describes three needs that were not being met, and which the refugees turned into thriving industries: the telephone linkage to hook up refugees with relatives in the West; the provision of water that was chronically short in the camp; and the construction of housing to replace tents. These needs were seen by entrepreneurial refugees as business opportunities and they started small businesses which also served the local community.

Throughout Africa, refugee camps that persist for more than a few years gradually turn into more permanent structures that come to resemble villages. There are brick or cement buildings and houses, roads, schools, health clinics that serve the entire host community, restaurants and coffee shops. Thriving street markets offer a multitude of goods, including illicit ones, that were unattainable in the region before. Refugee camps are by no means model villages; on the contrary, they are usually characterised by crime and insecurity, and refugees seek to leave them. But, in many host countries, the food security and education and health services in refugee camps are far better than those available to the local population. A well-known example is Kakuma camp, on the Sudan-Kenya border, where the poverty-stricken Turkana local population are considerably worse off than the Sudanese and other refugees in the camp, and are even employed by refugees to carry water, fetch firewood, provide child care and so on. In many countries, it is common for more vulnerable (and even less vulnerable) members of the local community to enter refugee camps and pass themselves off as refugees in order to gain access to assistance. Refugee camps can serve as places of assistance for local people in times of economic duress such as drought. For example, during the 1990s drought in eastern Ethiopia, a substantial number of the locals managed to get registered as refugees and benefited from the relief distribution (Kibreab 1993).

When refugees do not live in camps, but are self-settled amongst the host community, they provide economic inputs in the form of new technologies and skills, entrepreneurship or needed labour. Refugees can thus have a multiplier effect, by expanding the capacity and productivity of the receiving area's economy through local or even regional trade and the growth of markets. Some host countries have benefited economically from refugees as a result of agricultural expansion or intensification made possible by refugee labour or new farming practices. This has occurred in eastern Sudan Bascom 1998; Kok 1989), western Zambia (Bakewell 2000), and western Tanzania (Daley 1993), among other places. Local farmers can benefit when there is increased demand by refugees for local food (especially when the food aid provided by international organisations is unfamiliar and disliked). Trade (or barter) of food aid for local produce is common.

Since host communities are not economically homogeneous, the effects of these economic changes will vary for different groups (Bascom 1998; Chambers 1986). Inevitably, some groups will be marginalised, and others will gain disproportionately. However, this is an empirical issue and will vary in different contexts. What is clear is that refugees and refugee assistance are potentially able to make a contribution to the country's welfare and development, and can benefit the state accordingly.

Notes:

1. For a review of this literature see Jacobsen 2001. Some case studies include Bakewell 2000, Black 1994 and Hansen 1999 (Zambia); Bascom 1998 and Kibreab 1996 (Sudan); Callamard 1994 (Malawi).

2. It is common to see the World Food Programme's sacks of maize and soya oil as well as UNHCR's familiar blue tarpaulins for sale in local markets. In countries like Tanzania and Sudan, regional trading networks have developed based on food aid after it is trucked out of camps and local markets and transported to wholesale markets in towns in the region (Landau 2001)

3. Email communication with an NGO implementing partner in Zambia. Unfortunately the results of this initiative have just been pittances: so far only $5,000,000 has been forthcoming, meant to be spread over agriculture, education, health and road works.

4. In Tanzania, the author was present in June 1999, when the government and UNHCR were negotiating about the location for a new camp for Congolese refugees. The government argued for the camp to be constructed some miles south of Kigoma. Access to the new camp would have required the road along the lake to be upgraded, and a bridge built across a river. The road and bridge would have benefited the state because it is a primary trucking link between northwestern Tanzania and Zambia. UNHCR refused the location and one closer to existing Congolese camps was chosen. However the example illustrates the way in which host governments see relief organisations like UNHCR as potential sources of development for refugee receiving regions.

5. Under the project, some 7,700 refugees and people from nearby communities have received rice, ground nut and maize seeds as well as hoes and machetes. Trees are being

planted in former camps as well as existing ones. The project also entails helping local people near the camps to plant perennials such as coffee trees and oil palms. However there is a big gap between available funding and the amounts needed to repair the damage.

References:

Bakewell, O. 2000. 'Repatriation and self-settled refugees in Zambia: bringing solutions to the wrong problems', *Journal of Refugee Studies* 13, 4:356–73.

Bascom, J. 1998. *Losing Place: refugee populations and rural transformations in East Africa.* New York: Berghahn.

Bayart, J.-F., S. Ellis & B. Hibou. 1999. *The Criminalization of the State in Africa.* Oxford: James Currey.

Black, R. 1994. 'Refugee migration and local economic development in Eastern Zambia', *Journal of Economic and Social Geography* 85, 3.

Callamard, A. 1994. 'Refugees and local hosts: a study of the trading interactions between Mozambican refugees and Malawian villagers in the district of Mwanza', *Journal of Refugee Studies* 7, 1:39–62.

Chambers, R. 1986. 'Hidden losers? The impact of rural refugees and refugee programs on poorer hosts', *International Migration Review* 20, 2:245–63.

Crisp, J. 2000. 'A state of insecurity: the political economy of violence in refugee-populated areas of Kenya', *Refugee Studies Quarterly* 19, 1:54–70.

Daley, P. 1993. 'From the Kipande to the Kibali: the incorporation of refugees and labour migrants in Western Tanzania, 1900–1987', in R. Black & V. Robinson, eds., *Geography and Refugees: patterns and processes of change.* London: Belhaven Press.

de Waal, A. 1997. *Famine Crimes: politics and the disaster relief industry in Africa.* Oxford: James Currey.

Dick, S. 'Liberians in Ghana: living without humanitarian assistance', Recent Issues in Refugee Research, *UNHCR Working Paper No. 57.* <http://www.unhcr.ch/refworld/pubs/pubon.htm>

Goyens, P., D. Porignon, E. M. Soron'gane, R. Tonglet, P. Hennart & H. L. Vis. 1996. 'Humanitarian aid and health services in Eastern Kivu, Zaire: collaboration or competition?', *Journal of Refugee Studies* 9, 3:268–80.

Hansen, A. 1990. 'Refugee self-settlement versus settlement on government schemes', *Discussion Paper 17.* Geneva: UNRISD.

Herbst, J. 2000. *States and Power in Africa.* Princeton, NJ: Princeton University Press.

Jacobsen, K. 2000. 'A framework for exploring the political and security context of refugee populated areas', *Refugee Studies Quarterly* 19, 1:3–22.

Jacobsen, K. 2001. 'The forgotten solution: local integration for refugees in developing countries', New Issues in Refugee Research, *UNHCR Working Paper No. 45.* <http://www.unhcr.ch/refworld/pubs/pubon.htm>

Kaiser, T. 2000. 'UNHCR's withdrawal from Kiryandongo: anatomy of a handover', New Issues in Refugee Research, *UNHCR Working Paper No. 32.* <http://www.unhcr.ch/refworld/pubs/pubon.htm>

Kibreab, G. 1993. 'The myth of dependency among camp refugees', *Journal of Refugee Studies* 6, 4:321–49.

Kibreab, G. 1996. *People on the Edge in the Horn: displacement, land use & the environment in the Gedaref Region,* Sudan. Oxford: James Currey.

Kok, W. 1989. 'Self-settled refugees and the socio-economic impact of their presence on Kassala, Eastern Sudan', *Journal of Refugee Studies* 2, 4: 419–40.

Landau, L. B. 2001. 'The humanitarian hangover: transnationalization of governmental practice in Tanzania's refugee-populated areas', New Issues in Refugee Research, *UNHCR Working Paper No. 40*. <http://www.unhcr.ch/refworld/pubs/pubon.htm>

Moore, D. 2000. 'Humanitarian agendas, state reconstruction and democratisation processes in war-torn societies', New Issues in Refugee Research, *UNHCR Working Paper No. 24*. <http://www.unhcr.ch/refworld/pubs/pubon.htm>

Nicholson, F. & P. Twomey, 1999. *Refugee Rights and Realities: evolving international concepts and regimes.* Cambridge University Press.

Payne, L.1996. *Rebuilding communities in a Refugee Settlement: a casebook from Uganda.* Oxford: Oxfam Great Britain.

Rutinwa, B. 1999. 'Refugee protection and interstate security: lessons from the recent tensions between Burundi and Tanzania', Oxford, March. Draft.

Smock, D. R. 1997. 'Humanitarian assistance and conflict in Africa', <http://www.jha.sps.cam.ac.uk/a/a016.htm>, reposted on 4.7.1997.

Sperl, S. 2000. 'International refugee aid and social change in Northern Mali', New Issues in Refugee Research, *UNHCR Working Paper No. 22.* <http://www.unhcr.ch/refworld/pubs/pubon.htm>

Sphere Project. 1997. 'Part II: the minimum standards, health services', *Humanitarian Charter and Minimum Standards in Disaster Response Handbook* 1997, accessed at <http://www.sphereproject.org/handbook/health.htm>

UNHCR. 1997. *The State of the World's Refugees 1997–98: a humanitarian agenda.* New York: Oxford University Press.

UNHCR. 1999. *Handbook for Emergencies.* Geneva: UNHCR.

UNHCR Uganda. 1999. Strategy Paper: self reliance for refugee hosting areas, 1999–2003. Kampala: UNHCR Uganda, with Office of the Prime Minister.

Van Damme, W. 1995. 'Do refugees belong in camps? Experiences from Goma and Guinea', *The Lancet* 346: 360–6.

Weiss, T. G. & C. Collins, 1996. *Humanitarian Challenges and Intervention: world politics and the dilemmas of help.* Boulder, CO: Westview.

Weiss, T. G. & L. Gordenker. 1996. *NGOS, the UN, & Global Governance.* Boulder, CO: Lynne Rienner.

World Refugee Survey. 2001. Washington, DC: US Committee for Refugees.

TRC's Final Report: An In-Depth Look at the Implications

Semantics King Jr.

Semantics King Jr. is an African journalist and a former fellow of the World Press Institute. In the following viewpoint, he says that the release of the Truth and Reconciliation Commission (TRC) report has stirred up divisions and tensions in Liberia that were largely quieted. He worries that the effort to arrest former warlords, as recommended by the TRC, will result in renewed violence. He also discusses divisions among the people on the committee and suggests that these may undermine the authority of the report.

When the Liberian Transitional Legislative Assembly enacted the Truth and Reconciliation Commission Act in May 2005 to establish Liberia's Truth Commission, the Act tasked the TRC "to promote national peace, security, unity and reconciliation" by investigating gross human rights violations and violations of humanitarian law, sexual violations, and economic crimes that occurred between January 1979 and October 2003.

The Commission could also explore the period before 1979 as needed, and it (TRC) was also mandated to determine whether abuses were isolated incidents or part of a systematic pattern,

Semantics King, Jr., "TRC's Final Report: An In-Depth Look at the Implications," *New Liberian*/Community Renewal Society, July 9, 2009. Reproduced with permission.

establish the antecedents, circumstances, factors and context of such violations and abuses, and determine those responsible for the commission of the violations, their motives as well as the impact of the abuses on victims. Additionally, the Commission was mandated to provide a forum against impunity, establish the record of the past and compile a public report with findings and recommendations.

Therefore, in fulfillment of that mandate, the TRC last Tuesday released its final report containing findings, determinations and recommendations made by the Commission to the National Legislature.

But exactly one week after the report was made public to the Liberian citizenry and the International community, there have been reactions both for and against the final report by many Liberians who themselves were victims of the civil war.

What is also interesting is that when the first volume of the TRC's final report was released in December last year, there were not many rancors among Liberians. But now that the volume two report has been released and recommendations made for probable prosecution of those responsible for the carnage and mayhem caused Liberia and Liberians, the country has even become more divided than it was during the height of the civil war.

The division stems from the fact, among other pertinent issues, that the current Liberian leader, Ellen Johnson Sirleaf, is among several Liberians recommended to be banned from running or holding public office for thirty years.

By that recommendation, it seems president Sirleaf might be ineligible for a re-run for president come 2011 should the country's National Legislature adopt the recommendations from the TRC.

Some Liberians are even of the view that the TRC did a disservice to Liberia's post-war reconciliation drive. At issue also is that eight former Liberian war Lords, including former president Charles Taylor, have been recommended for prosecution.

Consequently, former war Lord, now lecturer of Mass Communication at the University of Liberia, Alhaji G.V. Kromah has questioned the transparency of the report. Mr. Kromah, speaking to the BBC in Monrovia outlined these questions for the TRC: "What is the integrity of the process? How did you come to the conclusions? Who are you? Did you use competent means? Explain to the public, what methodology did you use? We know in law what is admissible. Did you depend on hearsay? Did you depend on prejudice? Then you want to push to conclusions. Then you will have injustice."

Except for some legal issues, but many of Mr. Kromah's questions can be answered by even a competent well-informed 9th grade Liberian student. Liberians know who the TRC are. They saw the process and so Mr. Kromah's questions, as much as he might have had a point, seem irrelevant given that at issue now is how Liberians would handle such a fragile situation in a country that is just about recovering from war.

Although TRC Chairman Cllr Jerome Verdier, Sr has told the International community that most of what they did is part of what they (Commissioners) already knew, it is very important that we tread with caution regarding these recommendations. We have gone through the entire report page by page and realistically speaking, the findings and recommendations hold semblance of truth in them.

However, what is going to happen to Liberia should the National Legislature adopt the recommendations? Consider the potential for reeling into violence again should the former war Lords say they will fight anybody that would attempt to arrest them as one of them, Nimba county senator Prince Johnson is reported to have indicated. Will Liberia really see peace that Liberians are yearning for?

Possibly. But if there are any arrests to be made for prosecutions, the International community will have to help in the process. Like they (International Community) played a key role in arresting and turning Charles Taylor over to the International

Criminal Court for Sierra Leone, they will have to help with arresting all of them and prosecute them. One after the other.

Now that the TRC's mandate has officially ended on June 22, 2009 it is very important to commend the people that helped the process succeed. Despite all the challenges and criticisms from a cross section of the Liberian people, the TRC tried everything humanly possible to ensure that Liberians know all those who have helped to destroy the country.

As with anything, human nature is very hard to please. Liberians are an interesting set of people on the African continent. And as hard as you may try to please them, they will always find fault with you. But especially in politics, everybody has a stake. Imagine two commissioners, Cllr Pearl Brown Bull and Sheik Kafumba Konneh of the TRC publicly insinuating that the TRC's final report is null and void simply because they did not append their signatures to it?

Well, that's Liberia. However, the TRC members had this for their colleagues and Liberians: "We want to inform the Liberian people that diversity of opinions among the Commissioners does not undermine the credibility of the TRC Report, but rather lend credence to its contents. Furthermore, there is no law in the Commission's mandate and rules and procedures stating that the absence of the signatures of one or two Commissioners renders a particular decision invalid. As a matter of fact the Rules and Procedures of the Commission calls for a 2/3 majority vote to arrive at decisions."

The TRC added that "The mandate empowered the TRC to among other things address the issue of impunity pursuant to Article 7 Section 26, D of the TRC Act and to recommend prosecutions in particular cases as deemed appropriate, while Article 10 says the commission can recommend prosecution. We firmly believe that the report of the Commission is in no way contrary to its mandate."

A press release from the TRC today states that "We therefore seize this opportunity to express our disappointment and regret over the way, manner, and form in which the TRC Report and the recommendations are being politicized by two commissioners, Pearl Brown-Bull and Sheik Kafumba Konneh and their political and former factional allies. This ugly act by the Commissioners Bull and Konneh, which include feeding the public with half truths and false information has the propensity to derail the recommendations and endanger the lives of some respectable men and women who served this nation through the TRC."

What is also raising eye brows is that fact that the TRC even said today that its commissioners were distancing themselves from "the activities of these Commissioners (Bull and Konneh), who from the onset have worked to destroy the TRC process."

Now, if these honorable commissioners have worked to destroy the TRC process, then why keep them with the TRC? These commissioners were appointed and could be replaced. But since they remained in the employ of the Liberian people, although their actions and inactions proved that they were out there to destroy the TRC and by extension, Liberia and yet they were allowed to do their schemes, in effect, it means that the work of the TRC is questionable.

If all those associated with former warring factions, their leaders, political decision makers, financiers, organizers, commanders, and foot soldiers are prosecuted or barred from political office for thirty years, it means that Liberia stands a chance of getting new breed of leaders who would take the country to new dimensions providing that they do not practice what they saw their fore-runners doing for the better part of Liberia's national existence. But if they do follow in their footsteps, then Liberia truly is doomed for life.

Why am I saying this? The truth is that Liberia has a huge pool of young talents from across this globe and their experiences living abroad and in dangerous times back home would be a good CV for leadership in a country where everybody feels that the resources of the land are elephant meat for anybody to just grab and eat at the expense of the poor and under-represented.

And if the Liberian people don't go about this TRC report with care, only time could tell what awaits Liberia and Liberians again especially after the UN peacekeepers shall have been gone for real out of Liberia.

CHAPTER 3

Personal Narratives

Chapter Exercises

1. Writing Prompt

Imagine that you were a servant in an Americo-Liberian household immediately after Samuel K. Doe's coup. Write a journal entry describing your reactions and the reactions of your employers.

2. Group Activity

Form groups and develop five interview questions that could be used in conducting oral histories of child soldiers during the Liberian/Sierra Leone conflict.

Liberia: Mixed Feelings About Truth Commission's Purpose

IRIN

IRIN is a United Nations news service focusing on humanitarian stories in regions lacking such coverage. In the following viewpoint, IRIN reports on the feelings of both war victims and war combatants toward the (then) recently established Truth and Reconciliation Commission. This commission has refused to grant amnesty and has retained the right to recommend prosecutions. Many victims do not want to forgive, and many combatants do not want to come forward with their stories.

MONROVIA, 10 January 2008 (IRIN)—Many Liberians observing the opening of the country's first public truth and reconciliation commission hearings on 8 January were confused about what the hearings would mean if the accused would not be prosecuted afterwards.

Priscilla Hayner, an expert at the International Centre for Transitional Justice (ICTJ) in Geneva said it is "normal" in post-conflict environments that people doubt the importance of speaking collectively about war at first. She said that once the TRC's final report is drawn up attitudes might change.

IRIN, "Liberia: Mixed Feelings About Truth Commission's Purpose," January 10, 2008. Copyright © 2008 by IRIN. All rights reserved. Reproduced by permission.

"The story is still being written. It's true that in some countries the public does take a cynical and untrusting approach to the process, but then at the end the report can be extraordinarily powerful. Sometimes it goes the other way and after a great investigation the Commission struggles to get it on paper." The TRC has faced a hard slog in Liberia, trying to match very high expectations with few resources, Hayner noted. However Anthony Valke, Liberia head of the American Bar Association, an international non-governmental organisation working on judicial reform in Liberia, said the public's interest in the TRC is too low for it to count. "From our perspective, the TRC has not been able to properly carry out a robust information campaign about its role that would target perpetrators and guarantee amnesty to those perpetrators who are willing to come up and tell their stories." Valke said the TRC's refusal to guarantee amnesty and its unusual step of retaining the right to recommend prosecutions will dissuade most former fighters from attending. "Most of them are scared to come forward as the TRC and the government is not clear about amnesty for them," he said. IRIN spoke with several victims of the war and former fighters and what follows are excerpts of their testimonials.

Abu Dorley, Victim

"It is difficult for me to accept an apology from someone who brutally killed five of my family members—my mother, father and three sisters—before my very eyes in 1991. I want this person who committed the acts to be put on trial for atrocities because of the trauma he has caused in my life.

"The rebel fighter who did the killings still moves freely in Monrovia as if he has not committed any atrocity. I do not believe the TRC public hearing of my testimony will solve the pain and trauma I have been going through."

Miatta Momoh, Victim

One child soldier killed all 19 of Momoh's cousins in northern Liberia in 1995.

"There is no guarantee from the TRC that those who killed our families, loved ones and friends, raped our mothers and sisters, burnt down our villages and towns will be brought to justice as is the case with former President Charles Taylor now on trial in the Hague.

"This child soldier is now in the new Liberian Police Force. Our other family members in Monrovia can not easily forgive him unless he is tried."

Abraham Suah, Victim
Rebel fighters killed Suah's seven month pregnant wife at the start of the civil war in 1989.

"Just telling a victim sorry is a recipe for another round of atrocities as those perpetrators could do the same acts again in the future and rely on apologies, but when one is tried and convicted of war crimes, it would serve as deterrent to others."

Shad Sherman, Former Rebel
"As a former fighter, I know how most of my friends feel. They regret their actions and most of us are afraid to reach out to those who we wronged during the war, unless it is within a framework like the hearings which are sanctioned by government.

"Because I am afraid of what would happen to me I cannot personally go a particular family whose house I burnt down during the war. So the hearing will be good for me to meet them at the TRC forum."

Abel Peckor, Former Government Soldier
"All fighters decided to cease fire, disarm and move on with our lives and not repeat the mistake of taking up weapons against our own people.

"We are all striving for survival and if people begin pointing fingers at us, then we will be stigmatised and our hopes for survival will be dampened. No one will want to deal with us."

A Liberian Woman Remembers Fleeing Liberia as a Refugee

Louise Géesedeh Barton

Louise Géesedeh Barton was born in Liberia, from where she escaped as a refugee during the 1990 war. The following viewpoint describes her escape by boat to Guinea. She remembers the difficult boat crossing and a humiliating strip search by the authorities in Guinea. She concludes with a description of almost being refused asylum by the Guinean authorities. Barton currently lives in Atlanta, Georgia.

Eighty-seven souls, and their belongings, crammed as tightly as possible into an oversized canoe with one small outboard motor. A captain and two crewmembers manned it. I looked at the boat and wondered how it could possibly be seaworthy with the load it was to carry.

The Voyage

The boat had eight narrow benches that each sat five to six passengers, if they hunched their shoulders sideways. Five or six others sat on the floor between each bench. We four were fortunate

Louise Géesedeh Barton, *So Far to Run: The Memoir of Liberian Refugee Louise Géesedeh Barton*, Bascom Hill Publishing Group, 2012, pp. 200–206. Reproduced with permission.

enough to secure bench seating. Abel sat on my right, Moses and Cecelia on my left.

After everyone was onboard the captain hospitably announced, "Welcome aboard the Atlantic shuttle from Lungi to Guinea. This trip will take us the good part of two days. I have made hundreds of trips traveling these waters over the past eighteen years. I have never lost a single soul, and I don't plan to change that any time soon."

Before we pulled away he added, "We are expecting good weather for the entire trip, and if we are lucky you will be able to see some ocean life up close and personal." I cringed at that thought. The captain added, "Please do not stand up while we are underway, and keep your hands and other body parts inside the boat at all times."

The wooden boat creaked as it rocked gently back and forth on the waves that were washing up with slaps against its sides. The captain untied the dock lines and stepped into the boat. A couple of swift yanks on the pull rope, and the motor sputtered and started up. We edged away from the wharf and were under way.

We headed out for deep water as we watched the Lungi International Airport disappear from sight. The loud pulse of the motor, the wind blowing in our faces, and the occasionally drenching ocean spray kept me awake and alert. In silence, I prayed for God's protection and braced myself for the long and highly anticipated journey.

Three hours into the trip, after we had left the protection of the shore, a storm began forming. The wind began to blow in gusts. The waves rose, and broke over the bow of the pam-pam. It was rapidly taking on water. The once clear sky continued darkening, the clouds became heavy, the wind blew more steadily, and the waves grew much higher. Their tops blew off into spray that whipped at our faces. Most of us could not swim, and none of us had life preservers. Fearing the boat would capsize and sink, the majority of the passengers cried out to the captain that they wanted him to turn back. I cried out to God, "Please save us.

Have mercy—Lord—stop the storm, calm the waves. We can't turn back. We must find refuge in Guinea."

The captain steered the boat into the oncoming waves to keep us from rolling over. He screamed out over the wind, "I am the master of the sea! I know all the secrets of the ocean! We will be fine—trust me!"

Without mercy, our small, overloaded vessel was battered. Most of the passengers were panic-stricken and seasick, and each lurch and roll of the boat caused them to empty the contents of their stomachs and their bowels alternately all over themselves and the boat. The waves crashing down on us blended and splashed the vile mixture, causing those who were not sick from the motion to join in the misery. We might have lost a few passengers in the tumult if we had not packed ourselves into the boat so tightly. Parents held onto their children and merchants tried to keep their baskets and bags from washing overboard. . . .

Land, but Not Safety

A low rumble of weakened cheers arose from the passengers when land appeared on the horizon. The moment we pulled into the dock a small band of soldiers rushed over and demanded that we get out of the boat. We were relieved to step onto something that did not move, even though almost three days in a small boat made many of us sway from side-to-side as we walked, causing us to look as if we were drunk.

For some reason, the soldiers singled out and brutally beat some of the passengers. The rest of us could only huddle together in shock and confusion, hoping we would not receive the same treatment.

The commanding officer ordered. "Have all these people stripped and searched!" Guinean soldiers stood by with their rifles in their hands to enforce his command. Men, women, and children all stripped in one large group. Their methods of search and interrogation were cruel and unusual. The soldiers manhandled men as well as women during the process, irreverently

Liberian refugees line up for gasoline rations at a refugee camp in southeastern Guinea in 2004. More than 25,000 Liberians fled their country during the 2002–2003 conflict. © Alexandre Grosbois/AFP/Getty Images.

poking, prodding, and even fondling us, under the pretense of looking for rebel markings.

Ongoing bouts of sickness still came in waves over those who were ill. Abel was one of them, and he was suffering terribly; I was afraid for him. Finally, at the end of the long, drawn-out strip search, the Coast Guard Captain felt satisfied that we were all innocent passengers. Since it was getting dark, he announced he would escort us to Conakry in the morning.

The local people had heard that the Coast Guard had captured and arrested a band of rebels, but once they realized we were not rebels, they took pity on us and offered assistance. A kindly woman waved at our little group of four and said in French, "*Venez ici,*" meaning, "Come here." She guided us to her small cinder-block home, where she boiled water in a large pot so we could scour off the filth that covered us after our difficult voyage. She made a large pot of fish soup and while we were eating, she compounded an herbal remedy to help Abel, who had apparently contracted cholera from one of the passengers.

To Conakry, Guinea

In the morning, our captain and crew tried to remove the drying effluence that clung to the benches and insides of the boat, but they did not have sufficient time to do a thorough job. Worn-out, haggard, and sickly passengers formed a disorderly line at the dock. Their pallid countenances revealed their persisting illness. I supported Abel as much as I could. He had become so weak that he had great difficulty making it out onto the dock and could barely stand while waiting to board the *pam-pam.*

Those in front of us began inching their way forward ever so slowly. The crewmembers gave a hand to the weak and infirm as they boarded. We scrunched as closely to each other as we could and exchanged queasy looks, pinched smiles, and tight but hopeful nods.

For the next three hours, the Guinean Coast Guard escorted us toward Conakry. Each minute seemed like an eternity. The boat began to fill again with sea spray and more uncontrolled eliminations by the passengers. The captain finally announced that we had entered the waters off Conakry. We were elated and rejoiced at knowing we would soon disembark and be free to contact the UN for assistance. The Coast Guard motioned for us to continue on our way without escort, and our captain was again in charge of our voyage.

After five more difficult hours, we entered a small, shallow harbor at Boussoura Port in Conakry. As we neared a low, concrete wharf, designed to accommodate the many pam-pams that surrounded it, a *pam-pam* filled with immigrations officers made its way toward us. The officer in charge shouted, "Who's the captain?" Our captain waved his hand and replied, "I am." Fearing he might be carrying rebels, the officer said, "You are overloaded. There are too many males onboard. You must return to Lungi."

Our captain knew the immigrations officer as well as most of the *pam-pam* captains in the harbor. It seemed to frustrate him that the immigrations officer apparently did not trust him. Our captain tried to stay calm, but, in his exasperation, he answered tersely, "We've already been stopped by the Guinea Coast Guard, and my passengers were subjected to a humiliating strip search. They determined that my passengers are not rebels and they escorted us here. Many of my passengers have become critically ill and require medical attention." The officer waved us away, ignoring our captain's pleas, again ordering us to leave the harbor and return to Lungi. At this point, other passengers joined me in begging the officer to reconsider. Our voices rose together as we implored him for our very lives.

Our captain entreated, "We will all die at sea, we do not have enough food, water, or fuel for the journey." He added, "Even if I did have enough fuel, as you can see my passengers are very sick, and I might lose some of them."

At this point, a young man, one of the many who plied the shallow water bare-backed and in cutoff shorts offering themselves for hire to run errands or to load cargo, came near our boat. The tide was out and the water was shallow enough for him to be only waist deep. Our captain called to him, asking him to take a fuel can and some money to buy fuel for us.

Another Storm

The immigrations officer did not interfere and gave the order for his small vessel to return to the wharf. Our captain had dropped an anchor by this time and he got out of the boat in order to follow the immigrations boat so he could continue trying to make sense to the officer.

During all this confusion of negotiations for fuel, wailings of the passengers, and yelling back and forth between our captain and the immigrations officer, another storm had begun to brew. As we waited, the pleasant weather rapidly deteriorated into a violent storm with hurricane-force gusts and driving rain. Even in the shallow water, the wind churned up enormous waves that tossed the boat violently. Screams of terror from the passengers blended with the howling of the wind and our boat began to fill with water so fast that there was no doubt it would sink.

The roof of the small, harbor-side guard post ripped off and those on the wharf and on shore ran for cover as flying objects tumbled past them. Someone in authority yelled out. "Get those people out of the water. Bring them in!" Our *pam-pam* had filled so much with water, though, that it could not make way on its own, and another boat hurried out to rescue us.

By the time the rescue boat arrived, our boat was nearly submerged. We were completely awash and our belongings were being carried out of the boat with each new wave. There was no way to wade ashore; the waves would have knocked us under. The wind and waves were so strong that as passengers stood up to transfer to the other boat they tumbled backward into ours. Somehow, we all managed to scramble aboard the rescue boat and made for the wharf.

The moment we got off the boat, the men received orders to form one line and the women another and we hurried into the Security/Customs facility. The officer in charge scowled and looked our way. He pointed at the line of men, said something gruffly in French, which he translated, "The women and children can stay. All the men must return at once to Sierra Leone."

Although a few of the men were merchants and had not brought their wives on the trip, the major portion of our group was couples having the sole intent of escaping the civil war and finding refuge in Guinea. The women protested and begged the officer to allow the men to stay. Everyone pointed out how ill they were, too ill to survive a return voyage.

We were relieved when, after a long debate, the officials finally reconsidered and the officer in charge said, "Okay, the men may stay as long as they have their papers. Please proceed."

A Liberian Woman Remembers Being a Rebel Soldier

Diane Taylor

Diane Taylor is a freelance journalist who focuses on human rights. In the following viewpoint, she profiles Black Diamond, a Liberian woman who joined the rebel troops after being raped by Charles Taylor's forces. Taylor relates Diamond's satisfaction at the former Liberian president's conviction of war crimes. She also discusses the difficulty Diamond has had adjusting to peacetime, in part because of the stigma faced by former fighters. Though Diamond remains proud of her role in the fighting and of her refusal to be a victim, she sees war as terrible and hopes for lasting peace in Liberia.

Black Diamond has never met Charles Taylor, but she still calls the day the former Liberian president was sentenced for crimes against humanity the happiest of her life. On Wednesday [in May 2012], Taylor is expected to be sentenced for his crimes and the 30-year-old former female rebel leader who fought against him will be watching with interest.

Diane Taylor, "Black Diamond: A Female Victim of Charles Taylor's Crimes Speaks Out," *The Guardian*, May 28, 2012. Copyright © 2012 by The Guardian. All rights reserved. Reproduced with permission.

The Man Who Ruined Her Future

"This is the man who ruined my future," she says. "When I see him sentenced, maybe I will be able to move on. They say he will get 80 years. This will send an important message to the world that you can't do terrible things and just get away with it."

Taylor has been convicted of crimes including murder, rape and conscripting child soldiers in neighbouring Sierra Leone, but he wreaked havoc in his own country too. More than 200,000 people were killed in Liberia's 14-year civil war, countless girls and women were raped and much of the population was displaced.

Black Diamond was 18 and a promising student when civil war broke out. She enjoyed a peaceful childhood in Voinjama, a town in the north of the country where her father worked as a doctor. During one of Taylor's troops' regular raids, in April 2000, her parents were killed and Diamond was gang-raped.

After regaining consciousness after the attack, she found her way to the headquarters of Sekou Conneh, the leader of Liberians United for Reconciliation & Democracy (Lurd) and begged him to take her in. When the compound was attacked soon after she arrived, she simply grabbed an AK-47 and joined in with the fighting.

Rising swiftly through the ranks Diamond became a colonel in Lurd's Women's Auxiliary Corps, developing a reputation as a ferocious fighter. Many of the women were, like her, survivors of rape by Taylor's troops and many had come to the conclusion that becoming a fighter was the best way to protect themselves against further rapes. Diamond still refers to them fondly as her "girls." Of the 12 she fought closely with, six died in the course of the war. "Becoming a fighter was the best thing I could do under the circumstances," she says now. But she remains haunted by all the horrors she witnessed.

By all accounts, Diamond struck fear into the hearts of her opponents during the war, boldly wielding her AK-47 and staring death in the face without flinching. Yet in person she is quiet, almost diffident, her dark eyes downcast. In war she had a role:

Colonel Black Diamond (right, wearing sunglasses), and her bodyguards wait at a checkpoint before going on patrol in 2003. Former fighters like her continue to face stigma. © Georges Gobet/AFP/Getty Images.

in peace, like many ex-combatants, she has struggled to reinvent herself. Ex-combatants are stigmatised in Liberian society and this attitude compounds her despair.

Never Another War

"I am suffering today because of what Charles Taylor did. The war took everything from me: my parents, my education and my future. I want to spread the message that we must pursue peace. We must make sure that we never see another war here in Liberia."

Today she lives in a small, overcrowded place in the middle of the Liberian capital Monrovia, a city still bearing the physical scars of war and teeming with poverty-stricken people struggling to make a living. The water supply is uncertain, rats are a perennial problem and hunger is ever-present.

Black Diamond is one of the 85% of her country's population living below the poverty line. She is a single parent caring for her two young children and three others who lost family members during the war. The children are plagued by bouts of malaria and her attempts to find a stable job have been unsuccessful.

She supports the work of the country's president Ellen Johnson Sirleaf, who has tried hard to unite the Liberians, despite once supporting Taylor, as well as fellow Nobel prize winner and peace campaigner Leymah Gbowee. Yet she supports the actions of her "girls." "Liberian women have always been strong and we are proud to have the first female president in Africa. Before the war, rape was almost unknown in our country. When the rapes started, I and the other girls who fought were determined not to be victims. We wanted to fight back to show our attackers they couldn't get away with such things and that they, not we, should feel shame for the rapes."

She welcomes the opportunity to work with anyone who can help her spread the message of peace to try to protect the next generation from the horrors she experienced. "I am doing this for my girls," she says. "Those who are lost and those who are living presently."

Liberians in Minnesota Tell Stories of Abuse, Torture

Toni Randolph

Toni Randolph is an editor for Minnesota Public Radio. In the following viewpoint, she interviews Liberians in Minnesota who have provided statements about their experiences to the Truth and Reconciliation Commission. Randolph talks in particular to two women: Williametta Saydee, who discusses her experiences at the beginning of the civil war in 1990, and Yende Anderson, the granddaughter of former Liberian president William Tolbert, Jr., who discusses the torture of her father following the 1980 coup in which Tolbert was overthrown.

Twenty-nine year-old Williametta Saydee told the Truth and Reconciliation Commission about the day in 1990 when a band of young men came to her aunt's home in a rural area of Liberia. Saydee, who is among the first Liberians in Minnesota to put her story on the record, was about 12 years old at the time.

She was outside brushing her teeth because there was no longer any running water in her part of the country as a result of the

Toni Randolph, "Liberians in Minnesota Tell Stories of Abuse, Torture," MPRnews, May 1, 2007. From Minnesota Public Radio, copyright © 2007. All rights reserved. Reproduced with permission.

civil war. She says she wasn't paying much attention to the young men who called themselves "freedom-fighters"—until they shot and killed another man in cold blood.

Saydee and her aunt fled with eight cousins to the home of another family member. They passed through checkpoints on the hours-long walk and saw gruesome signs of the civil war.

"Between checkpoints, you'd see bodies littering the road. Bodies just littered the street. At that time, it was the first time I'd seen bodies in all stages of decomposition. Just killed, swollen up, (a) black person turning white and then dried up, down to the skeletal level. It was just a sad, sad time," she said.

Saydee's smile fades and she chokes up as she recalls the troubled time. But she says she found a silver lining in the telling of her story.

"Just talking about what had happened to me with people helped because afterwards, I felt sort of relieved. It was like I had a huge burden on my shoulder that I wasn't truly aware of and it had been lifted up," she said.

Saydee, who says her story is nothing compared to what others experienced, is encouraging all Liberians to tell their stories so they too, can feel a similar sense of relief.

During 16 years of civil war in Liberia, thousands of people were killed, tortured, imprisoned and raped. The Truth and Reconciliation Commission is investigating human rights abuses stemming from the fighting so that those responsible can be held accountable. In a first-of-its kind effort, the commission is taking testimony from Liberians, not just in the small west African country, but from those around the world. Census figures estimate about 7,000 Liberians live in Minnesota, although Liberians here say the community is much larger.

Thirty-two-year-old Yende Anderson told her family's story. She talked about what happened after her grandfather, former Liberian President William Tolbert, Jr., was assassinated in 1980. Anderson says her father, who had worked for her grandfather, was arrested, imprisoned and tortured.

"He went through a lot of suffering from the beatings. They were beaten with the rods from inside tires. He was stripped in public, made to eat human feces twice. If he didn't eat it they were going to shoot him. He dug his grave on several occasions, but they never killed him," she said.

Eventually her family was reunited and they moved to the United States in 1985. Anderson says lifting personal burdens is important, but there's even more to be gained.

"For this to work, I think you can help people heal, but more importantly, it can lay a foundation of what went wrong and how we can prevent it," she said.

The statements are being taken by dozens of volunteers in the Twin Cities, many of them lawyers who are donating their time. One of them, Dulce Foster with the law firm Fredrikson and Byron, says she's heard about some awful experiences, but she's been impressed with the Liberians she's met.

"I haven't sat down with any Liberian who hasn't had something absolutely horrific to tell me. And yet to be able to put aside the bitterness and anger that might come from that and the emotional damage that might come from that and say, 'we want to put down our arms,' that's a courageous thing," she said.

The Liberian Truth and Reconciliation Commission will collect statements through the end of the year. So far, about 200 Liberians in Minnesota have either told their story or registered to do so. The commission will begin taking statements in other parts of the United States in June.

Organizations to Contact

The editors have compiled the following list of organizations concerned with the issues debated in this book. The descriptions are derived from materials provided by the organizations. All have publications or information available for interested readers. The list was compiled on the date of publication of the present volume; the information provided here may change. Be aware that many organizations take several weeks or longer to respond to inquiries, so allow as much time as possible.

Amnesty International
5 Penn Plaza, 14th Floor
New York, NY 10001
(212) 807-8400 • fax: (212) 463-9193
e-mail: aimember@aiusa.org
website: www.amnestyusa.org

Amnesty International is a worldwide movement of people who campaign for internationally recognized human rights. Its vision is of a world in which every person enjoys all of the human rights enshrined in the Universal Declaration of Human Rights and other international human rights standards. Each year it publishes a report on its work and its concerns throughout the world.

Embassy of Liberia
5201 16th Street NW
Washington, DC 20011
(202) 723-0437 • fax: (202) 775-5365
e-mail: info@embassyofliberia.org
website: www.liberianembassyus.org

The Embassy of Liberia is the country's official diplomatic representative in the United States. The embassy's website includes information and articles on Liberia and United States/Liberia relations, and Liberia's foreign policy, news, and press releases.

Friends of Liberia (FOL)
1812 Monroe Street NW
Washington, DC 20010
(202) 643-0428
e-mail: Liberia@fol.org
website: http://fol.org

FOL is a nongovernmental, nonprofit organization that seeks to positively affect Liberia by supporting education, social, economic and humanitarian programs, and through advocacy efforts. Its website includes news and events, back issues of the FOL newsletter, and information about FOL's projects.

Global Witness
529 14th Street NW, Suite 1085
Washington, DC 20045
(202) 621-6665
e-mail: mail@globalwitness.org
website: www.globalwitness.org

Global Witness investigates and campaigns to prevent natural resource–related conflict and corruption as well as associated environmental and human rights abuses using undercover investigations, lobbying, and advocacy. The Global Witness website includes many articles and reports on the relationship between the timber industry and historical violence in Liberia and West Africa.

Human Rights First
333 Seventh Avenue, 13th Floor
New York, NY 10001-5108
(202) 845-5200 • fax: (212) 845-5399
e-mail: feedback@humanrightsfirst.org

website: www.humanrightsfirst.org

Human Rights First is an independent advocacy and action organization that presses the US government and private companies to respect human rights and the rule of law. It also develops policy solutions to support human rights. Its website includes press releases, news, and reports on human rights issues around the world.

Human Rights Watch
350 Fifth Avenue
34th Floor
New York, NY 10118-3299
(212) 290-4700 • fax: (212) 736-1300
e-mail: hrwnyc@hrw.org
website: www.hrw.org

Founded in 1978, this nongovernmental organization conducts systematic investigations of human rights abuses in countries around the world. It publishes many books and reports on specific countries and issues as well as annual reports and other articles. Its website includes numerous discussions of human rights and international justice issues.

International Center for Transitional Justice (ICTJ)
5 Hanover Square, Floor 24
New York, NY 10004
(917) 637-3800
e-mail: info@ictj.org
website: www.ictj.org

ICTJ works to help societies in transition address the legacy of human rights violations. Working with international organizations, governments, victim's groups, and activists, it provides technical expertise and knowledge of relevant comparable experiences in transitional justice. It also researches, analyzes, and reports on transitional justice developments worldwide.

Montreal Institute for Genocide and Human Rights Studies
Concordia University
1455 De Maisonneuve Boulevard West
Montreal, Quebec, H3G 1M8, Canada
(514) 848-2424, ext. 5729 or 2404 • fax: (514) 848-4538
website: http://migs.concordia.ca

MIGS, founded in 1986, monitors native language media for early warning signs of genocide in countries deemed to be at risk of mass atrocities. The institute houses the Will to Intervene (W2I) Project, a research initiative focused on the prevention of genocide and other mass atrocity crimes. The institute also collects and disseminates research on the historical origins of mass killings and provides comprehensive links to this and other research materials on its website. The website also provides numerous links to other websites focused on genocide and related issues, as well as to specialized sites organized by nation, region, or case.

STAND/United to End Genocide
1025 Connecticut Avenue, Suite 310
Washington, DC 20036
(202) 556-2100
e-mail: info@standnow.org
website: www.standnow.org

STAND is the student-led division of United to End Genocide (formerly Genocide Intervention Network). STAND envisions a world in which the global community is willing and able to protect civilians from genocide and mass atrocities. In order to empower individuals and communities with the tools to prevent and stop genocide, STAND recommends activities from engaging government representatives to hosting fundraisers, and has more than one thousand student chapters at colleges and high schools. While maintaining many documents online regarding genocide, STAND provides a plan to promote action as well as education.

United Human Rights Council (UHRC)
104 N. Belmont Street, Suite 313
Glendale, CA 91206
(818) 507-1933
e-mail: contact@uhrc.org
website: www.unitedhumanrights.org

The United Human Rights Council (UHRC) is a committee of the Armenian Youth Federation. By means of action on a grass-roots level, the UHRC works toward exposing and correcting human rights violations of governments worldwide. The UHRC campaigns against violators in an effort to generate awareness through boycotts, community outreach, and education. The UHRC website focuses on the genocides of the twentieth century.

List of Primary Source Documents

The editors have compiled the following list of documents that either broadly address genocide and persecution or more narrowly focus on the topic of this volume. The full text of these documents is available from multiple sources in print and online.

Convention Against Torture and Other Cruel, Inhuman, or Degrading Punishment, United Nations, 1974

A draft resolution adopted by the United Nations General Assembly in 1974 opposing any nation's use of torture, unusually harsh punishment, and unfair imprisonment.

Convention on the Prevention and Punishment of the Crime of Genocide, December 9, 1948

A resolution of the United Nations General Assembly that defines genocide in legal terms and advises participating countries to prevent and punish actions of genocide in war and peacetime.

Judgment of the Special Court for Sierra Leone in the Case of Charles Taylor, May 18, 2012

The Special Court for Sierra Leone details its finding that Charles Taylor was guilty of war crimes associated with the war in Sierra Leone.

Liberian Declaration of Independence, July 16, 1847

The document officially declaring Liberia's independence from the American Colonization Society, which had settled African Americans in the country. The Declaration is based on the American Declaration of Independence in many respects and also discusses the oppression of African Americans.

Nobel Lecture of Ellen Johnson Sirleaf, December 10, 2011

Ellen Johnson Sirleaf was one of the recipients of the Nobel Peace Prize in 2011; in her speech she talks about the progress of Liberia and the role of women in peace.

Principles of International Law Recognized in the Charter of the Nuremburg Tribunal, United Nations International Law Commission, 1950

After World War II (1939–1945), the victorious allies legally tried surviving leaders of Nazi Germany in the German city of Nuremburg. The proceedings established standards for international law that were affirmed by the United Nations and by later court tests. Among other standards, national leaders can be held responsible for crimes against humanity, which might include "murder, extermination, deportation, enslavement, and other inhuman acts."

Rome Statute of the International Criminal Court, July 17, 1998

The treaty that established the International Criminal Court. It establishes the court's functions, jurisdiction, and structure.

United Nations General Assembly Resolution 96 on the Crime of Genocide, December 11, 1946

A resolution of the United Nations General Assembly that affirms that genocide is a crime under international law.

Universal Declaration of Human Rights, United Nations, 1948

Soon after its founding, the United Nations approved this general statement of individual rights it hoped would apply to citizens of all nations.

Whitaker Report on Genocide, 1985

This report addresses the question of the prevention and punishment of the crime of genocide. It calls for the establishment of an international criminal court and a system of universal jurisdiction to ensure that genocide is punished.

For Further Research

Books

Greg Campbell, *Blood Diamonds: Tracing the Deadly Path of the World's Most Precious Stones*. New York: Basic, 2012.

James Ciment, *Another America: The Story of Liberia and the Former Slaves Who Ruled It*. New York: Hill and Wang, 2013.

Leymah Gbowee and Carol Mithers, *Mighty Be Our Powers: How Sisterhood, Prayer, and Sex Changed a Nation at War*. New York: Beast, 2011.

Felix Gerdes, *Civil War and State Formation: The Political Economy of War and Peace in Liberia*. Frankfurt, Germany: Campus, 2013.

Danny Hoffman, *The War Machines: Young Men and Violence in Sierra Leone and Liberia*. Durham, NC: Duke University Press, 2011.

Alcinda Honwana, *Child Soldiers in Africa*. Philadelphia: University of Pennsylvania Press, 2011.

Agnes Kamara-Umunna and Emily Holland, *And Still Peace Did Not Come: A Memoir of Reconciliation*. New York: Hyperion, 2011.

Ellen Johnson Sirleaf, *This Child Will Be Great: Memoir of a Remarkable Life by Africa's First Woman President*. New York: HarperCollins Publishers, 2009.

Colin M. Waugh, *Charles Taylor and Liberia: Ambition and Atrocity in Africa's Lone Star State*. London, England: Zed, 2012.

Gabriel I.H. Williams, *Liberia: The Heart of Darkness*. Victoria, British Columbia: Trafford, 2002.

Periodicals

"After Liberia's Wars, A Forum For Forgiveness," NPR, March 22, 2011. www.npr.org.

Dio Appleton, "On 1979 Rice Riot: PAL Gave President Tolbert $20,000," *Liberian Journal,* August 15, 2008. http://theliberianjournal.com.

Associated Press, "Liberian President Charles Taylor Serves 50-Year Sentence in British Prison," *Washington Post,* October 10, 2013. www.washingtonpost.com.

Helene Cooper, "On Day of Reckoning, Recalling Horror That Swallowed Liberia," *New York Times,* April 26, 2012. www.nytimes.com.

Alexander Barnes Dryer, "Our Liberian Legacy," *The Atlantic,* July 30, 2003. www.theatlantic.com.

"The Betrayal of Samuel K. Doe and the Howler That Worsened the Liberian War: What Lessons as ECOMOG Moves into Another Theatre of Chaos and Carnage?," *Cocorioko,* February 10, 2013. www.cocorioko.net.

Leon Dash, "Liberian Soldiers Taunt, Shoot 13 Former Leaders," *Washington Post,* April 23, 1980. www.washingtonpost.com.

Colin Freeman, "Blood Diamonds and Charles Taylor: The Inside Story," *The Telegraph,* August 15, 2010. www.telegraph.co.uk.

James W. Harris, "Have Liberians Squandered Opportunity to Reconcile Their Nation?," *Liberian Journal,* June 12, 2013. http://theliberianjournal.com.

Sarah Left, "War in Liberia," *The Guardian,* August 4, 2003. www.theguardian.com.

"Liberia: Ex-President Samuel Doe's Children Step into the Limelight, Call for Genuine Reconciliation and Unity,

Invite Mrs. Quiwonkpa as Keynote Speaker of Program Celebrating Life of Late Father," *New Dispensation,* February 27, 2012. http://thenewdispensation.com.

"Liberia: Opinion Divided on Truth and Reconciliation Findings," IRIN, July 6, 2009. www.irinnews.org.

Kylin Navarro, "Liberian Women Act to End Civil War, 2003," Global Nonviolent Action Database, October 22, 2010. http://nvdatabase.swarthmore.edu.

Esther Pan, "Liberia: Child Soldiers," *Council on Foreign Relations,* August 29, 2003. www.cfr.org.

Mary K. Ricks, "Was Liberia Founded By US Slaves?," *Salon,* July 3, 2003. www.slate.com.

Shamara Riley, "Former American Slaves Played Oppressive Role in Liberia's Past," *The Grio,* February 1, 2010. http://thegrio.com

Ellen Johnson Sirleaf interviewed by Johnny Dwyer, "The New Iron Lady," *Foreign Policy,* October 2, 2013. www.foreignpolicy.com.

Christopher Tuck, "'Every Car or Moving Object Gone': The ECOMOG Intervention in Liberia," *African Studies Quarterly,* vol. 4, no. 1, 2000. www.africa.ufl.edu.

US Department of State, "Liberian Refugees in West Africa," www.state.gov.

Finlay Young, "Lost Boys: What Became of Liberia's Child Soldiers?," *The Independent,* April 14, 2002. www.independent.co.uk.

Laura A. Young and Rosalyn Park, "Engaging Diasporas in Truth Commissions: Lessons from the Liberia Truth and Reconciliation Commission Diaspora Project," *International Journal of Transitional Justice,* vol. 3, no. 3, 2009, pp. 341–361.

Websites and Films

Pray the Devil Back to Hell (2008). Directed by Gini Reticker, produced by Abigail Disney. This documentary is about the Women of Liberia Mass Action for Peace. The movement was organized by social worker Leymah Gbowee in Monrovia. It enacted nonviolent protests involving singing and praying in an effort to end Liberia's war.

The Trial of Charles Taylor (www.charlestaylortrial.org). This website covers the day-to-day events of the trial of Charles Taylor in The Hague, the Netherlands. It is intended both to help West African journalists trying to cover the trial and to inform the public. Posts are provided by Alpha Sesay, a Sierra Leonean lawyer.

Truth and Reconciliation Commission of Liberia (http://trcofliberia.org). The official website of the Truth and Reconciliation Commission of Liberia (TRC) includes the full TRC reports, news, transcripts from the hearing, and other information pertaining to the Liberian conflict, war crimes, and human rights violations.

Index

NORTH COTTAGE HIGH SCHOOL
5704 - 60th Street
Red Deer, AB T4N 6V6
403-342-2170